2022 SUPPLEMENT TO

CONSTITUTIONAL LAW

CASES, COMMENTS, AND QUESTIONS

Thirteenth Edition

■ ■ ■

Jesse H. Choper

Earl Warren Professor of Public Law (Emeritus)
University of California, Berkeley

Michael C. Dorf

Robert S. Stevens Professor of Law
Cornell University

Richard H. Fallon, Jr.

Story Professor of Law
Harvard Law School

Frederick Schauer

David and Mary Harrison Distinguished Professor of Law
University of Virginia

AMERICAN CASEBOOK SERIES®

WEST
ACADEMIC
PUBLISHING

American Casebook Series is a trademark registered in the U.S. Patent and Trademark Office.

© 2020, 2021 LEG, Inc. d/b/a West Academic
© 2022 LEG, Inc. d/b/a West Academic
      444 Cedar Street, Suite 700
      St. Paul, MN 55101
      1-877-888-1330

West, West Academic Publishing, and West Academic are trademarks of West Publishing Corporation, used under license.

Printed in the United States of America

ISBN: 978-1-63659-923-6

TABLE OF CONTENTS

TABLE OF CASES

The principal cases are in bold type.

_____

TABLE OF AUTHORITIES

2022 SUPPLEMENT TO

CONSTITUTIONAL LAW

CASES, COMMENTS, AND QUESTIONS

Thirteenth Edition

CHAPTER 1

NATURE AND SCOPE OF JUDICIAL REVIEW

■ ■ ■

2. POLITICAL QUESTIONS

P. 41, after *Nixon v. United States*:

RUCHO V. COMMON CAUSE
588 U.S. ___, 139 S.Ct. 2484, 204 L.Ed.2d 931 (2019).

CHIEF JUSTICE ROBERTS delivered the opinion of the Court.

Voters and other plaintiffs in North Carolina and Maryland challenged their States' congressional districting maps as unconstitutional partisan gerrymanders. The North Carolina plaintiffs complained that the State's districting plan discriminated against Democrats; the Maryland plaintiffs complained that their State's plan discriminated against Republicans. The plaintiffs alleged that the gerrymandering violated the First Amendment, the Equal Protection Clause of the Fourteenth Amendment, the Elections Clause, and Article I, § 2, of the Constitution.

[All agree that the partisan gerrymanders at issue in the two cases were deliberate and at least initially highly effective. In *Rucho*, the North Carolina case] one of the two Republicans chairing the redistricting committee [explained] that the map was drawn with the aim of electing ten Republicans and three Democrats because he did "not believe it [would be] possible to draw a map with 11 Republicans and 2 Democrats." One Democratic state senator objected that entrenching the 10–3 advantage for Republicans was not "fair, reasonable, [or] balanced" because, as recently as 2012, "Democratic congressional candidates had received more votes on a statewide basis than Republican candidates." [In] November 2016, North Carolina conducted congressional elections using the 2016 Plan [at issue in the litigation], and Republican candidates won 10 of the 13 congressional districts.

[The] second case before us is *Lamone v. Benisek*. In 2011, the Maryland Legislature—dominated by Democrats—undertook to redraw the lines of that State's eight congressional districts. The Governor at the time, Democrat Martin O'Malley, [appointed] a redistricting committee to help redraw the map. [The] Governor later testified that his aim was to "use the redistricting process to change the overall composition of

Maryland's congressional delegation to 7 Democrats and 1 Republican by flipping" one district. [The] 2011 Plan accomplished that by moving roughly 360,000 voters out of the Sixth District and moving 350,000 new voters in. Overall, the Plan reduced the number of registered Republicans in the Sixth District by about 66,000 and increased the number of registered Democrats by about 24,000. The map was adopted by a party-line vote. It was used in the 2012 election and succeeded in flipping the Sixth District. A Democrat has held the seat ever since.

[In] these cases we are asked to decide an important question of constitutional law. "But before we do so, we must find that the question is presented in a 'case' or 'controversy' that is, in James Madison's words, 'of a Judiciary Nature.' " *DaimlerChrysler Corp. v. Cuno*, 547 U.S. 332, 342 (2006) (quoting 2 Records of the Federal Convention of 1787, p. 430 (M. Farrand ed. 1966)). [The] question here is whether there is an "appropriate role for the Federal Judiciary" in remedying the problem of partisan gerrymandering—whether such claims are claims of *legal* right, resolvable according to *legal* principles, or political questions that must find their resolution elsewhere.

Partisan gerrymandering is nothing new. Nor is frustration with it. [The] Framers addressed the election of Representatives to Congress in the Elections Clause. Art. I, § 4, cl. 1. That provision assigns to state legislatures the power to prescribe the "Times, Places and Manner of holding Elections" for Members of Congress, while giving Congress the power to "make or alter" any such regulations. [The Court here cited historical examples of congressional regulation before recognizing that only a requirement that states use single-member districts remains in place today.]

[Appellants] suggest that, through the Elections Clause, the Framers set aside electoral issues such as the one before us as questions that only Congress can resolve. We do not agree. In two areas—one-person, one-vote and racial gerrymandering—our cases have held that there is a role for the courts with respect to at least some issues that could arise from a State's drawing of congressional districts. See *Wesberry v. Sanders*, 376 U.S. 1 (1964); *Shaw v. Reno*, 509 U.S. 630 (1993).

But the history is not irrelevant. The Framers were aware of electoral districting problems and considered what to do about them. [At] no point was there a suggestion that the federal courts had a role to play. Nor was there any indication that the Framers had ever heard of courts doing such a thing.

[Partisan] gerrymandering claims have proved far more difficult to adjudicate [than one-person, one-vote cases and cases involving racial discrimination]. The basic reason is that, while it is illegal for a jurisdiction to depart from the one-person, one-vote rule, or to engage in racial discrimination in districting, "a jurisdiction may engage in constitutional political gerrymandering." *Hunt v. Cromartie*, 526 U.S. 541, 551 (1999) (citing *Bush v. Vera*, 517 U.S. 952, 968 (1996)).

To hold that legislators cannot take partisan interests into account when drawing district lines would essentially countermand the Framers' decision to entrust districting to political entities. The "central problem" is not determining whether a jurisdiction has engaged in partisan gerrymandering. It is "determining when political gerrymandering has gone too far." *Vieth* [*v. Jubelirer*, 541 U.S. 267, 296 (2004) (plurality opinion). The Court here recounted its prior confrontations will challenges to political gerrymandering. In *Davis v. Bandemer*, 478 U.S. 109 (1986)), a majority thought the case was justiciable but splintered over the proper standard to apply. Four Justices (White, Brennan, Marshall, and Blackmun, JJ.) would have required proof of "intentional discrimination against an identifiable political group and an actual discriminatory effect on that group." Two Justices (Powell and Stevens, JJ.) would have focused on "whether the boundaries of the voting districts have been distorted deliberately and arbitrarily to achieve illegitimate ends." But O'Connor, J., joined by Burger, C.J., and Rehnquist, J., would have held that partisan gerrymandering claims pose political questions because the Equal Protection Clause simply "does not supply judicially manageable standards for resolving" them.]

[Eighteen years later, in *Vieth*, Justice Scalia's plurality opinion also would have held challenges to gerrymanders nonjusticiable due to an absence of judicially manageable standards.] Kennedy, J., concurring in the judgment, noted "the lack of comprehensive and neutral principles for drawing electoral boundaries [and] the absence of rules to limit and confine judicial intervention." He nonetheless left open the possibility that "in another case a standard might emerge." Four Justices dissented.

[The] question [in appraising political gerrymandering claims] is one of degree: How to "provid[e] a standard for deciding how much partisan dominance is too much." *League of United Latin American Citizens v. Perry*, 548 U.S. 399, 420 (2006) (opinion of Kennedy, J.). And it is vital in such circumstances that the Court act only in accord with especially clear standards: "With uncertain limits, intervening courts—even when proceeding with best intentions—would risk assuming political, not legal, responsibility for a process that often produces ill will and distrust." *Vieth*, 541 U.S., at 307 (opinion of Kennedy, J.).

[Partisan] gerrymandering claims invariably sound in a desire for proportional representation. * * * "Our cases, however, clearly foreclose any claim that the Constitution requires proportional representation." [Unable] to claim that the Constitution requires proportional representation outright, plaintiffs inevitably ask the courts to make their own political judgment about how much representation particular political parties *deserve*—based on the votes of their supporters—and to rearrange the challenged districts to achieve that end. But federal courts are not equipped to apportion political power as a matter of fairness, nor is there any basis for concluding that they were authorized to do so.

[The] initial difficulty in settling on a "clear, manageable and politically neutral" test for fairness is that it is not even clear what fairness looks like in this context. [Fairness] may mean a greater number of competitive districts. [On] the other hand, perhaps the ultimate objective of a "fairer" share of seats in the congressional delegation is most readily achieved by yielding to the gravitational pull of proportionality and engaging in cracking and packing, to ensure each party its "appropriate" share of "safe" seats. [Or] perhaps fairness should be measured by adherence to "traditional" districting criteria, such as maintaining political subdivisions, keeping communities of interest together, and protecting incumbents.

[Deciding] among just these different visions of fairness (you can imagine many others) poses basic questions that are political, not legal. There are no legal standards discernible in the Constitution for making such judgments, let alone limited and precise standards that are clear, manageable, and politically neutral.

[Even] assuming the court knew which version of fairness to be looking for, there are no discernible and manageable standards for deciding whether there has been a violation. [Appellees] contend that if we can adjudicate one-person, one-vote claims, we can also assess partisan gerrymandering claims. [But] "vote dilution" in the one-person, one-vote cases refers to the idea that each vote must carry equal weight. [That] requirement does not extend to political parties. It does not mean that each party must be influential in proportion to its number of supporters.

Appellees and the dissent propose a number of "tests" for evaluating partisan gerrymandering claims, but none meets the need for a limited and precise standard that is judicially discernible and manageable. And none provides a solid grounding for judges to take the extraordinary step of reallocating power and influence between political parties.

[The District Court in the North Carolina case used a test that involved a "predominant" legislative purpose coupled with a demand for] a showing "that the dilution of the votes of supporters of a disfavored party in a particular district [is] likely to persist in subsequent elections such that an elected representative from the favored party in the district will not feel a need to be responsive to constituents who support the disfavored party."

[The] District Court's "predominant intent" prong is borrowed from the racial gerrymandering context. [If] district lines were drawn for the purpose of separating racial groups, then they are subject to strict scrutiny because "race-based decisionmaking is inherently suspect." But determining that lines were drawn on the basis of partisanship does not indicate that the districting was improper. A permissible intent—securing partisan advantage—does not become constitutionally impermissible, like racial discrimination, when that permissible intent "predominates."

The District Court tried to limit the reach of its test by requiring plaintiffs to show, in addition to predominant partisan intent, that vote dilution "is likely to persist" to such a degree that the elected representative will feel free to ignore the concerns of the supporters of the minority party. But "[t]o allow district courts to strike down apportionment plans on the basis of their prognostications as to the outcome of future elections . . . invites 'findings' on matters as to which neither judges nor anyone else can have any confidence." *Bandemer*, 478 U.S., at 160 (opinion of O'Connor, J.).

[The] District Courts also found partisan gerrymandering claims justiciable under the First Amendment, coalescing around a basic three-part test: proof of intent to burden individuals based on their voting history or party affiliation; an actual burden on political speech or associational rights; and a causal link between the invidious intent and actual burden. [To] begin, there are no restrictions on speech, association, or any other First Amendment activities in the districting plans at issue. [The] plaintiffs' argument is that partisanship in districting should be regarded as simple discrimination against supporters of the opposing party on the basis of political viewpoint. [It] provides no standard for determining when partisan activity goes too far.

As for actual burden, the slight anecdotal evidence found sufficient by the District Courts in these cases shows that this too is not a serious standard for separating constitutional from unconstitutional partisan gerrymandering. [How] much of a decline in voter engagement is enough to constitute a First Amendment burden? How many door knocks must go unanswered? How many petitions unsigned? How many calls for volunteers unheeded

The dissent proposes using a State's own districting criteria as a neutral baseline from which to measure how extreme a partisan gerrymander is. The dissent would have us line up all the possible maps drawn using those criteria according to the partisan distribution they would produce. Distance from the "median" map would indicate whether a particular districting plan harms supporters of one party to an unconstitutional extent.

As an initial matter, it does not make sense to use criteria that will vary from State to State and year to year as the baseline for determining whether a gerrymander violates the Federal Constitution. The degree of partisan advantage that the Constitution tolerates should not turn on criteria offered by the gerrymanderers themselves.

[Even] if we were to accept the dissent's proposed baseline, it would return us to "the original unanswerable question (How much political motivation and effect is too much?)." *Vieth*, 541 U.S., at 296–297 (plurality opinion). Would twenty percent away from the median map be okay? Forty percent? Sixty percent? Why or why not?

[The] dissent argues that there are other instances in law where matters of degree are left to the courts. True enough. But those instances typically involve constitutional or statutory provisions or common law confining and guiding the exercise of judicial discretion. [Here], on the other hand, the Constitution provides no basis whatever to guide the exercise of judicial discretion. [The] only provision in the Constitution that specifically addresses the matter assigns it to the political branches. See Art. I, § 4, cl. 1. [The Court next dismissed arguments based on the Elections Clause and Article I, § 2.]

Excessive partisanship in districting leads to results that reasonably seem unjust. But the fact that such gerrymandering is "incompatible with democratic principles," does not mean that the solution lies with the federal judiciary. [Federal] judges have no license to reallocate political power between the two major political parties, with no plausible grant of authority in the Constitution, and no legal standards to limit and direct their decisions.

[Our] conclusion does not condone excessive partisan gerrymandering. Nor does our conclusion condemn complaints about districting to echo into a void. The States, for example, are actively addressing the issue on a number of fronts. [The Court here described state legislation, state ballot initiatives, and state constitutional amendments to limit partisan gerrymandering.]

[As] noted, the Framers gave Congress the power to do something about partisan gerrymandering in the Elections Clause. [The Court here described several bills introduced in Congress.] We express no view on any of these pending proposals. We simply note that the avenue for reform established by the Framers, and used by Congress in the past, remains open.

* * *

JUSTICE KAGAN, with whom JUSTICES GINSBURG, BREYER, and SOTOMAYOR join, dissenting.

For the first time ever, this Court refuses to remedy a constitutional violation because it thinks the task beyond judicial capabilities. [The] partisan gerrymanders in these cases deprived citizens of the most fundamental of their constitutional rights: the rights to participate equally in the political process, to join with others to advance political beliefs, and to choose their political representatives. [If] left unchecked, gerrymanders like the ones here may irreparably damage our system of government. And checking them is *not* beyond the courts. The majority's abdication comes just when courts across the country, including those below, have coalesced around manageable judicial standards to resolve partisan gerrymandering claims.

[The] majority concedes (really, how could it not?) that gerrymandering is "incompatible with democratic principles." [That] recognition would seem to demand a response. The majority offers two ideas * * *. One is that the political process can deal with the problem—a proposition so dubious on its face that I feel secure in delaying my answer for some time. The other is that political gerrymanders have always been with us. To its credit, the majority does not frame that point as an originalist constitutional argument. After all (as the majority rightly notes), racial and residential gerrymanders were also once with us, but the Court has done something about that fact. The majority's idea instead seems to be that if we have lived with partisan gerrymanders so long, we will survive.

That complacency has no cause. [While] bygone mapmakers may have drafted three or four alternative districting plans, today's mapmakers can generate thousands of possibilities at the touch of a key—and then choose the one giving their party maximum advantage (usually while still meeting traditional districting requirements). The effect is to make gerrymanders far more effective and durable than before, insulating politicians against all but the most titanic shifts in the political tides.

[Partisan] gerrymandering of the kind before us not only subverts democracy (as if that weren't bad enough). It violates individuals' constitutional rights as well. [That] practice implicates the Fourteenth Amendment's Equal Protection Clause. [And] partisan gerrymandering implicates the First Amendment too. That Amendment gives its greatest protection to political beliefs, speech, and association. Yet partisan gerrymanders subject certain voters to "disfavored treatment"—again, counting their votes for less—precisely because of "their voting history [and] their expression of political views." *Vieth*, 541 U.S., at 314 (opinion of Kennedy, J.).

[The] majority never disagrees; it appears to accept the "principle that each person must have an equal say in the election of representatives." And indeed, without this settled and shared understanding that cases like these inflict constitutional injury, the question of whether there are judicially manageable standards for resolving them would never come up.

So the only way to understand the majority's opinion is as follows: In the face of grievous harm to democratic governance and flagrant infringements on individuals' rights—in the face of escalating partisan manipulation whose compatibility with this Nation's values and law no one defends—the majority declines to provide any remedy. [I'll] give the majority this one—and important—thing: It identifies some dangers everyone should want to avoid. Judges should not be apportioning political power based on their own vision of electoral fairness, whether proportional representation or any other. And judges should not be striking down maps left, right, and center, on the view that every smidgen of politics is a smidgen too much. Respect for state legislative processes—and restraint in the exercise of judicial authority—counsels intervention in only egregious cases.

But in throwing up its hands, the majority misses something under its nose: What it says can't be done *has* been done. Over the past several years, federal courts across the country—including, but not exclusively, in the decisions below—have largely converged on a standard for adjudicating partisan gerrymandering claims (striking down both Democratic and Republican districting plans in the process).

[Start] with the standard the lower courts used. [B]oth courts (like others around the country) used basically the same three-part test to decide whether the plaintiffs had made out a vote dilution claim. As many legal standards do, that test has three parts: (1) intent; (2) effects; and (3) causation. First, the plaintiffs challenging a districting plan must prove that state officials' "predominant purpose" in drawing a district's lines was to "entrench [their party] in power" by diluting the votes of citizens favoring its rival. [Justice Kagan here cited *Common Cause v. Rucho*, 318 F. Supp. 3d 777, 805–806 (M.D.N.C. 2018).] Second, the plaintiffs must establish that the lines drawn in fact have the intended effect by "substantially" diluting their votes. [Justice Kagan here cited *Benisek v. Lamone*, 348 F. Supp. 3d 493, 498 (Md. 2018).] And third, if the plaintiffs make those showings, the State must come up with a legitimate, non-partisan justification to save its map. If you are a lawyer, you know that this test looks utterly ordinary. It is the sort of thing courts work with every day.

[The] majority's response to the District Courts' purpose analysis is discomfiting. The majority does not contest the lower courts' findings; how could it? Instead, the majority says that state officials' intent to entrench their party in power is perfectly "permissible," even when it is the predominant factor in drawing district lines. But that is wrong. [W]hen political actors have a specific and predominant intent to entrench themselves in power by manipulating district lines, that goes too far.

[On] to the second step of the analysis, where the plaintiffs must prove that the districting plan substantially dilutes their votes. [Consider] the sort of evidence used in North Carolina first. There, the plaintiffs demonstrated the districting plan's effects mostly by relying on what might be called the "extreme outlier approach." [The] approach—which also has recently been used in Michigan and Ohio litigation—begins by using advanced computing technology to randomly generate a large collection of districting plans that incorporate the State's physical and political geography and meet its declared districting criteria, *except for* partisan gain. [The] further out on the tail, the more extreme the partisan distortion and the more significant the vote dilution.

Using that approach, the North Carolina plaintiffs offered a boatload of alternative districting plans—all showing that the State's map was an out-out-out-outlier. One expert produced 3,000 maps, adhering in the way described above to the districting criteria that the North Carolina redistricting committee had used, other than partisan advantage. To calculate the partisan outcome of those maps, the expert also used the same election data (a composite of seven elections) that [a North Carolina expert] had employed when devising the North Carolina plan in the first instance. [Every] single one of the 3,000 maps would have produced at least one more Democratic House Member than the State's actual map, and 77% would have elected three or four more. [Based] on those and other findings, the District Court determined that the North Carolina plan substantially dilutes the plaintiffs' votes.

Because the Maryland gerrymander involved just one district, the evidence in that case was far simpler—but no less powerful for that. [In] the old Sixth [District], 47% of registered voters were Republicans and only 36% Democrats. But in the new Sixth, 44% of registered voters were Democrats and only 33% Republicans. That reversal of the district's partisan composition translated into four consecutive Democratic victories, including in a wave election year for Republicans (2014). In what was once a party stronghold, Republicans now have little or no chance to elect their preferred candidate. The District Court thus found that the gerrymandered Maryland map substantially dilutes Republicans' votes.

[By] substantially diluting the votes of citizens favoring their rivals, the politicians of one party had succeeded in entrenching themselves in office. They had beat democracy.

The majority's broadest claim, as I've noted, is that this is a price we must pay because judicial oversight of partisan gerrymandering cannot be "politically neutral" or "manageable." [Consider] neutrality first. Contrary to the majority's suggestion, the District Courts did not have to—and in fact did not—choose among competing visions of electoral fairness. That is because they did not try to compare the State's actual map to an "ideally fair" one (whether based on proportional representation or some other criterion). Instead, they looked at the difference between what the State did and what the State would have done if politicians hadn't been intent on partisan gain. Or put differently, the comparator (or baseline or touchstone) is the result not of a judge's philosophizing but of the State's own characteristics and judgments.

[The] majority's sole response misses the point. According to the majority, "it does not make sense to use" a State's own (non-partisan) districting criteria as the baseline from which to measure partisan gerrymandering because those criteria "will vary from State to State and year to year." But that is a virtue, not a vice—a feature, not a bug.

[The] majority's "how much is too much" critique fares no better than its neutrality argument. How about the following for a first-cut answer: This much is too much. By any measure, a map that produces a greater partisan skew than any of 3,000 randomly generated maps (all with the State's political geography and districting criteria built in) reflects "too much" partisanship. Think about what I just said: The absolute worst of 3,001 possible maps. The *only one* that could produce a 10–3 partisan split even as Republicans got a bare majority of the statewide vote. And again: How much is too much? This much is too much: A map that without any evident non-partisan districting reason (to the contrary) shifted the composition of a district from 47% Republicans and 36% Democrats to 33% Republicans and 42% Democrats. A map that in 2011 was responsible for the largest partisan swing of a congressional district in the country.

And if the majority thought that approach too case-specific, it could have used the lower courts' general standard—focusing on "predominant" purpose and "substantial" effects—without fear of indeterminacy. I do not take even the majority to claim that courts are incapable of investigating whether legislators mainly intended to seek partisan advantage.

[Nor] is there any reason to doubt, as the majority does, the competence of courts to determine whether a district map "substantially" dilutes the votes of a rival party's supporters from the everything-but-partisanship baseline described above. [As] this Court recently noted, "the law is full of instances" where a judge's decision rests on "estimating rightly . . . some matter of degree"—including the "substantial[ity]" of risk or harm.

[This] Court has long understood that it has a special responsibility to remedy violations of constitutional rights resulting from politicians' districting decisions. [The] need for judicial review is at its most urgent in cases like these. "For here, politicians' incentives conflict with voters' interests, leaving citizens without any political remedy for their constitutional harms." [*Gill v. Whitford*, 138 S.Ct. 1916, 1941 (2018),] (Kagan, J., concurring). Those harms arise because politicians want to stay in office. No one can look to them for effective relief.

[Here Kagan, J., argued that Congress and state political processes were unlikely to provide an effective remedy After noting that the majority had also recognized state courts as a possible source of relief—since the political question doctrine does not apply to them—she asked:] But what do those courts know that this Court does not? If they can develop and apply neutral and manageable standards to identify unconstitutional gerrymanders, why couldn't we?

[The] practices challenged in these cases imperil our system of government. Part of the Court's role in that system is to defend its foundations. None is more important than free and fair elections. With respect but deep sadness, I dissent.

P. 44, substitute for note 3:

The topic of "judicially manageable standards" is extensively discussed and debated in *Rucho v. Common Cause*, which appears immediately above in this Supplement.

3. CONGRESSIONAL REGULATION OF JUDICIAL POWER

P. 60, at the end of note 9:

Department of Homeland Security v. Thuraissigiam, 140 S.Ct. 1959 (2020), found that a statute precluding habeas corpus review did not violate the Suspension Clause as applied to a noncitizen, apprehended within twenty-five yards of his initial crossing of the U.S. border, who sought to challenge administrative determinations that he had failed to establish a "credible fear of persecution" if returned to his homeland. Alito, J.'s, opinion for the Court reasoned that because the petitioner did not seek a "traditional" release from custody—but rather a "new opportunity to apply for asylum," during the pendency of which he would have remained in detention—he fell outside the scope of the writ as it existed when the Constitution was adopted. The Court also held that the denial of judicial review did not violate the Due Process Clause in the case of an alien who had neither lawfully entered the United States nor established significant contacts here. Breyer, J., joined by Ginsburg, J., concurred on the narrower ground that even if the petitioner would have had a right to habeas review of some issues bearing on the legality of his detention under the immigration laws, that right would not extend to claims as fact-bound as his. Sotomayor, J., joined by Kagan, J., dissented, affirming that the Suspension Clause entitled the petitioner to review of his claim that administrative officials had applied the wrong legal standard to his case.

CHAPTER 2

NATIONAL LEGISLATIVE POWER

■ ■ ■

3. THE NATIONAL TAXING AND SPENDING POWERS

I. REGULATION THROUGH TAXING

P. 143, at the end of note 1:

These questions were presented in CALIFORNIA v. TEXAS, 141 S.Ct. 2104 (2021), but the Court, in an opinion by BREYER, J., did not decide them on the ground that the plaintiffs lacked standing.

ALITO, J., joined by Gorsuch, J. dissented and would have reached the merits to find that zeroing out the tax rendered the mandate unconstitutional: "Congress cannot supplement its powers through the two-step process of passing a tax and then removing the tax but leaving in place a provision that is otherwise beyond its enumerated powers."

Is that the best characterization of what Congress did? Consider Michael C. Dorf, *Challengers to the Affordable Care Act Lose their Third Supreme Court Case: Will They Bring a Fourth?*, VERDICT (June 22, 2021), verdict.justia.com/2021/06/22/challengers-to-the-affordable-care-act-lose-their-third-supreme-court-case: "The post-2017 version of the ACA gives people a choice: buy health insurance [or] don't if you don't want to. [And] Congress undoubtedly has the power to instruct people that they don't have to do anything."

5. APPLYING NATIONAL POWERS TO STATE GOVERNMENTS: INTERGOVERNMENTAL IMMUNITIES

III. FEDERAL IMMUNITY FROM STATE TAXES

P. 166, at the end of footnote 85:

In *United States v. Washington*, 142 S.Ct. 1976 (2022), the Court unanimously found a constitutional violation despite a federal statutory waiver of immunity because the waiver applied to "generally applicable state workers' compensation laws" but did not "clearly and unambiguously authorize a State to enact a discriminatory law that facially singles out the Federal Government for unfavorable treatment" (internal quotation marks and citations omitted).

CHAPTER 3

DISTRIBUTION OF FEDERAL POWERS: SEPARATION OF POWERS

■ ■ ■

2. CONGRESSIONAL ACTION AFFECTING "PRESIDENTIAL" POWERS

I. DELEGATION OF RULEMAKING POWER

P. 221, before note 2:

(e) *Future of the "intelligible principle" test.* Congress enacted the Sex Offender Registration and Notification Act (SORNA), in order to provide for greater uniformity among state sex-offender registration systems, delegating to the Attorney General "the authority to specify the applicability of [its] requirements" to "offenders convicted before the enactment of" SORNA. In GUNDY v. UNITED STATES, 139 S.Ct. 2116 (2019), the Court rejected a nondelegation challenge to SORNA. KAGAN, J., announced the judgment of the Court and authored an opinion joined by three colleagues rejecting petitioner's contention that the Act "grants the Attorney General plenary power to determine SORNA's applicability to pre-Act offenders. [If] that were so, we would face a nondelegation question. But [the] Attorney General's discretion extends only to considering and addressing feasibility issues," thus satisfying the intelligible principle requirement.

Concurring only in the judgment, ALITO, J., agreed with that conclusion, adding that he would be willing to reconsider the post-*Schechter* nondelegation case law if a majority of the Court were to do so. GORSUCH, J., joined by Roberts, C.J., and Thomas, J., did not wish to wait. He dissented and would have reformed the doctrine by relying on a test that focuses on three questions: "Does the statute assign to the executive only the responsibility to make factual findings? Does it set forth the facts that the executive must consider and the criteria against which to measure them? And most importantly, did Congress, and not the Executive Branch, make the policy judgments? Only then can we fairly say that a statute contains the kind of intelligible principle the Constitution demands." KAVANAUGH, J., did not participate in *Gundy*.

P. 223, at the end of note 3(c):

In NATIONAL FEDERATION OF INDEP. BUS. v. DEP'T OF LABOR, OCCUPATIONAL SAFETY AND HEALTH ADMIN., 142 S.Ct. 661 (2022), the

Court, in a per curiam opinion, ruled that plaintiffs challenging a COVID-19 vaccine mandate for employers with more than 100 employees were likely to succeed on the merits on the ground that the mandate exceeded the scope of the statutory authority Congress had granted to the agency. Concurring, GORSUCH, J., joined by Thomas and Alito, JJ., contended that if the statute did confer on the agency "the power it asserts, that law would likely constitute an unconstitutional delegation of legislative authority." BREYER, J., joined by Sotomayor and Kagan, JJ., dissented.

In WEST VIRGINIA v. ENVIRONMENTAL PROTECTION AGENCY, 142 S.Ct. 2587 (2022), the Court, per ROBERTS, C.J., invoked the major questions doctrine, which it characterized as implementing "separation of powers principles," to conclude that Congress had not sufficiently clearly delegated to the EPA authority to impose caps on carbon emissions based on the premise that existing coal-fired power plants would shift their means of energy production to a less carbon-intensive source (such as natural gas) or participate in a cap-and-trade program. GORSUCH, J., joined by Alito, J, concurred, arguing that, absent judicial checks on agency action like the major questions doctrine, "[l]egislation would risk becoming nothing more than the will of the current President, or, worse yet, the will of unelected officials barely responsive to him." KAGAN, J., joined by Breyer and Sotomayor, JJ., dissented, contesting the majority's characterization of prior cases as establishing a distinctive major questions doctrine taking the form of a clear-statement rule: "in the relevant cases, the Court has done statutory construction of a familiar sort," looking "to the text of a delegation" and asking "whether Congress would naturally have delegated authority over some important question to the agency, given its expertise and experience."

III. APPOINTMENT AND REMOVAL OF OFFICERS

P. 254, before note 5:

(d) SEILA LAW LLC v. CONSUMER FINANCIAL PROTECTION BUREAU, 140 S.Ct. 2183 (2020), concerned a restriction on the President's power to remove the Director of the Consumer Financial Protection Bureau (CFPB) prior to the expiration of a five-year term. The Supreme Court, per ROBERTS, C.J., held the restriction unconstitutional:

"In the wake of the 2008 financial crisis, Congress [through the Dodd-Frank Act] established the [CFPB], an independent regulatory agency tasked with ensuring that consumer debt products are safe and transparent. In organizing the CFPB, Congress deviated from the structure of nearly every other independent administrative agency in our history. Instead of placing the agency under the leadership of a board with multiple members, Congress provided that the CFPB would be led by a single Director, who serves for a longer term than the President and cannot be removed by the President except for inefficiency, neglect, or malfeasance. The CFPB Director has no boss, peers, or voters to report to. Yet the Director wields vast rulemaking, enforcement, and adjudicatory authority over a significant portion of the U.S. economy. The question before us is whether this arrangement violates the Constitution's separation of powers.

"Our precedents have recognized only two exceptions to the President's unrestricted removal power. In *Humphrey's Executor* we held that Congress could create expert agencies led by a *group* of principal officers removable by the President only for good cause. And in *United States v. Perkins*, 116 U.S. 483 (1886) [which upheld tenure protections for a naval cadet-engineer], and *Morrison* we held that Congress could provide tenure protections to certain *inferior* officers with narrowly defined duties.

"We are now asked to extend these precedents to a new configuration: an independent agency that wields significant executive power and is run by a single individual who cannot be removed by the President unless certain statutory criteria are met. We decline to take that step. While we need not and do not revisit our prior decisions allowing certain limitations on the President's removal power, there are compelling reasons not to extend those precedents to the novel context of an independent agency led by a single Director. Such an agency lacks a foundation in historical practice and clashes with constitutional structure by concentrating power in a unilateral actor insulated from Presidential control."

The Court nonetheless denied relief to the petitioner, a California-based law firm that provided debt-related legal services to clients and that resisted a subpoena from the CFPB on the ground that, in light of the unconstitutional tenure protection for the Director, the agency had no lawful authority. In a portion of his lead opinion joined only by Alito and Kavanaugh, JJ., the Chief Justice rejected petitioner's plea: "The provisions of the Dodd-Frank Act bearing on the CFPB's structure and duties remain fully operative without the offending tenure restriction. Those provisions are capable of functioning independently, and there is nothing in the text or history of the Dodd-Frank Act that demonstrates Congress would have preferred *no* CFPB to a CFPB supervised by the President. Quite the opposite. [The] Dodd-Frank Act contains an express severability clause." Because the Justices who dissented on the merits concurred in the judgment with respect to severability, the petitioner was denied relief but the CFPB Director was rendered subject to removal at will by the President.

THOMAS, J., joined by Gorsuch, J., concurred in the merits: "*Humphrey's Executor* does not comport with the Constitution. [The] Constitution does not permit the creation of officers exercising 'quasi-legislative' and 'quasi-judicial powers' in 'quasi-legislative' and 'quasi-judicial agencies.' No such powers or agencies exist. Congress lacks the authority to delegate its legislative power, and it cannot authorize the use of judicial power by officers acting outside of the bounds of Article III. Nor can Congress create agencies that straddle multiple branches of Government. The Constitution sets out three branches of Government and provides each with a different form of power—legislative, executive, and judicial. [If] any remnant of *Humphrey's Executor* is still standing, it certainly is not enough to justify the numerous, unaccountable independent agencies that currently exercise vast executive power outside the bounds of our constitutional structure."

With respect to the remedy, THOMAS, J., joined by Gorsuch, J., dissented: "The Federal Judiciary does not have the power to excise, erase, alter, or otherwise strike down a statute. And the Court's reference to severability as a 'remedy' is inaccurate. Traditional remedies—like injunctions, declarations, or damages—operate with respect to specific parties, not on legal rules in the abstract [citations and internal quotation marks omitted]."

KAGAN, J., joined by Ginsburg, Breyer, and Sotomayor, JJ., concluded that "*if* the agency's removal provision is unconstitutional, it should be severed," but dissented on the merits: "The majority offers the civics class version of separation of powers—call it the Schoolhouse Rock definition of the phrase. [Yet,] as James Madison stated, the creation of distinct branches 'did not mean that these departments ought to have no partial agency in, or no controul over the acts of each other.' The Federalist No. 47. [The] founding era closed without any agreement that Congress lacked the power to curb the President's removal authority. And as it kept that question open, Congress took the first steps—which would launch a tradition—of distinguishing financial regulators from diplomatic and military officers. The latter mainly helped the President carry out his own constitutional duties in foreign relations and war. The former chiefly carried out statutory duties, fulfilling functions Congress had assigned to their offices. In addressing the new Nation's finances, Congress had begun to use its powers under the Necessary and Proper Clause to design effective administrative institutions. And that included taking steps to insulate certain officers from political influence. As the decades and centuries passed, those efforts picked up steam. Confronting new economic, technological, and social conditions, Congress—and often the President—saw new needs for pockets of independence within the federal bureaucracy. And that was especially so, again, when it came to financial regulation.

"[Congress's] choice to put a single director, rather than a multimember commission, at the CFPB's head violates no principle of separation of powers. [To] make sense on the majority's own terms, the distinction between singular and plural agency heads must rest on a theory about why the former more easily 'slip' from the President's grasp. But [the] opposite is more likely to be true: To the extent that such matters are measurable, individuals are easier than groups to supervise."

The Court relied on *Seila Law* in COLLINS v. YELLEN, 141 S.Ct. 1761 (2021), to invalidate the Federal Housing Finance Agency (FHFA), which is tasked by statute with supervising mortgage financing companies Fannie Mae and Freddie Mac. Congress placed the FHFA under a single Director removable by the President only "for cause." ALITO, J., spoke for the Court. Rejecting the contention that the FHFA's limited responsibilities relative to those of the CFPB distinguished *Seila Law*, he wrote that "the nature and breadth of an agency's authority is not dispositive in determining whether Congress may limit the President's power to remove its head. The President's removal power serves vital purposes even when the officer subject to removal is not the head of one of the largest and most powerful agencies."

SOTOMAYOR, J., joined by Breyer, J., dissented in part: "*Seila Law* did not hold that an independent agency may never be run by a single individual with tenure protection. Rather, that decision stated, repeatedly, that its holding was limited to a single-director agency with 'significant executive power.' "

Justices Thomas, Gorsuch, and Kagan joined in part by Breyer and Sotomayor, each wrote separately, concurring in whole or in part with the Court's remand for a determination of whether the removal restriction harmed the plaintiffs.

P. 257, after the carryover paragraph, insert the following:

UNITED STATES v. ARTHREX, INC., 141 S.Ct. 1970 (2021), per ROBERTS, C.J., was a successful challenge to the appointment of Administrative Patent Judges (APJs) responsible, among other things, for adjudicating the validity of previously issued patents when sitting in panels of the Patent Trial and Appeal Board. Although the Director of the Patent and Trademark Office, a principal officer, exercised significant control over APJs, who were appointed by the Secretary of Commerce and thus inferior officers, he lacked the ability to direct results: "Given the insulation of [their] decisions from any executive review, the President can neither oversee the [APJs] himself nor attribute [their] failings to those whom he *can* oversee. APJs accordingly exercise power that conflicts with the design of the Appointments Clause to preserve political accountability." (Citations and internal quotation marks omitted). In a portion of his opinion that spoke only for a plurality, the Chief Justice concluded that the proper remedy was to authorize the Director to review Board decisions, thus rendering APJs inferior officers. (To enable a coherent judgment, Breyer, J., who dissented from the substantive holding, joined the plurality's judgment with respect to the remedy.)

THOMAS, J., joined by Breyer, Sotomayor, and Kagan, JJ., dissented, pointing to various mechanisms by which the Director could exercise "functional power over" APJs. The Director sets APJ pay, "prescribes uniform procedural rules and formulates policies and procedures for Board proceedings, ... designate[s] and de-designate[s] Board decisions as precedential, [issues] binding policy directives that govern the Board." In addition, the Director "may release instructions that include exemplary applications of patent laws to fact patterns, which the Board can refer to when presented with factually similar cases. [He] may designate which of the 250-plus administrative patent judges hear certain cases and may remove administrative patent judges from their specific assignments without cause. [And] If the administrative patent judges (somehow) reach a result he does not like, the Director can add more members to the panel— including himself—and order the case reheard. [And if] the administrative patent judges (somehow) reach a result he does not like, the Director can add more members to the panel—including himself—and order the case reheard." (Citations and internal quotation marks omitted).

3. EXECUTIVE PRIVILEGE AND IMMUNITY

P. 267, replace (b) and (c) with the following:

(b) TRUMP v. VANCE, 140 S.Ct. 2412 (2020), addressed, in a criminal context, a question the Court specifically left open in *Clinton*: whether a sitting President enjoys any kind of immunity in actions in *state* court. A state prosecutor in New York City initiated a wide-ranging investigation and on behalf of a grand jury issued a subpoena *duces tecum* to an accounting firm seeking financial records of President Trump and his businesses beginning six years before and continuing into his presidency. The President argued that he enjoys absolute immunity from state criminal processes while in office. All nine members of the Court rejected the absolute immunity claim.

ROBERTS, C.J., wrote for the Court: "In our judicial system, 'the public has a right to every man's evidence.' Since the earliest days of the Republic, 'every man' has included the President of the United States. Beginning with Jefferson and carrying on through Clinton, Presidents have uniformly testified or produced documents in criminal proceedings when called upon by federal courts. This case involves—so far as we and the parties can tell—the first *state* criminal subpoena directed to a President. The President contends that the subpoena is unenforceable."

Chief Justice Roberts began by describing the long history of federal courts compelling, and of Presidents complying with, subpoenas, with special focus on the treason trial of Aaron Burr, at which Chief Justice Marshall, riding circuit, presided. *See United States v. Burr*, 25 F.Cas. 30 (CC Va. 1807). "Burr moved for a subpoena *duces tecum* directed at Jefferson. [The] prosecution opposed the request, arguing that a President could not be subjected to such a subpoena and that the [document Burr sought] might contain state secrets. [The] President, Marshall declared, does not 'stand exempt from the general provisions of the constitution.' [At] common law the 'single reservation' to the duty to testify in response to a subpoena was 'the case of the king,' whose 'dignity' was seen as 'incompatible' with appearing 'under the process of the court.' But, as Marshall explained, a king is born to power and can 'do no wrong.' The President, by contrast, is 'of the people' and subject to the law. According to Marshall, the sole argument for exempting the President from testimonial obligations was that his 'duties as chief magistrate demand his whole time for national objects.' But, in Marshall's assessment, those demands were 'not unremitting.' And should the President's duties preclude his attendance at a particular time and place, a court could work that out upon return of the subpoena. Marshall also rejected the prosecution's argument that the President was immune from a subpoena *duces tecum* because executive papers might contain state secrets. 'A subpoena duces tecum,' he said, 'may issue to any person to whom an ordinary subpoena may issue.' [In] the two centuries since the Burr trial, successive Presidents have accepted Marshall's ruling that the Chief Executive is subject to subpoena.

"[The President] argues that the Supremacy Clause gives a sitting President absolute immunity from state criminal subpoenas because compliance with those subpoenas would categorically impair a President's performance of his Article II functions. The Solicitor General, arguing on behalf of the United States, agrees with much of the President's reasoning but does not commit to his bottom line. Instead, the Solicitor General urges us to resolve this case by holding that a state grand jury subpoena for a sitting President's personal records must, at the very least, 'satisfy a heightened standard of need. . . .'

"[The President concedes] that state grand juries are free to investigate a sitting President with an eye toward charging him after the completion of his term. [His] objection therefore must be limited to the *additional* distraction caused by the subpoena itself. But that argument runs up against the 200 years of precedent establishing that Presidents, and their official communications, are subject to judicial process even when the President is under investigation.

"[The] President next claims that the stigma of being subpoenaed will undermine his leadership at home and abroad. Notably, the Solicitor General does not endorse this argument, perhaps because we have twice denied absolute immunity claims by Presidents in cases involving allegations of serious misconduct [citing Presidents Nixon and Clinton].

"[Finally,] the President and the Solicitor General [argue] that, while federal prosecutors are accountable to and removable by the President, the 2,300 district attorneys in this country are responsive to local constituencies, local interests, and local prejudices. [While] we cannot ignore the possibility that state prosecutors may have political motivations, [state and federal law] protect against the predicted abuse. [Moreover, t]he Supremacy Clause prohibits state judges and prosecutors from interfering with a President's official duties. [Any] effort to manipulate a President's policy decisions or to retaliate against a President for official acts through issuance of a subpoena would thus be an unconstitutional attempt to influence a superior sovereign exempt from such obstacles. We generally assume that state courts and prosecutors will observe constitutional limitations. Failing that, federal law allows a President to challenge any allegedly unconstitutional influence in a federal forum, as the President has done here [citations and internal quotation marks omitted].

"[Thus,] we cannot conclude that absolute immunity is necessary or appropriate under Article II or the Supremacy Clause. Our dissenting colleagues agree. [On] that point the Court is unanimous."

The Court next considered "whether a state grand jury subpoena seeking a President's private papers must satisfy a heightened need standard." It rejected such a standard "for three reasons. First, such a heightened standard would extend protection designed for official documents to the President's private papers. [Second,] heightened protection against state subpoenas is [not] necessary for the Executive to fulfill his Article II functions. [If] the state subpoena is not issued to manipulate, the documents themselves are not protected, and the Executive is not impaired, then nothing in Article II or the Supremacy Clause supports holding state subpoenas to a higher standard than their federal counterparts. Finally, in the absence of a need to protect the Executive, the public interest in fair and effective law enforcement cuts in favor of comprehensive access to evidence."

Having rejected the President's and Solicitor General's categorical arguments, the Court allowed the possibility of "subpoena-specific constitutional challenges" and accordingly remanded to the lower courts.

KAVANAUGH, J., joined by Gorsuch, J., concurred in the judgment. Agreeing with the Court's rejection of absolute immunity, he would have applied the "demonstrated, specific need" standard of *Nixon*, which he distinguished from the "heightened need" standard proposed by the Solicitor General: "The *Nixon* standard ensures that a prosecutor's interest in subpoenaed information is sufficiently important to justify an intrusion on the Article II interests of the Presidency [and] reduces the risk of subjecting a President to unwarranted burdens, because it provides that a prosecutor may obtain a President's information only in certain defined circumstances. Although the Court adopted the *Nixon* standard in a different Article II context—there, involving the confidentiality of official, privileged information—[there] are also important Article II (and Supremacy Clause) interests at stake here."

THOMAS, J., also wrote separately in what he styled a dissent, although he agreed with the Court that the President lacks "absolute immunity from *issuance* of the subpoena. But he may be entitled to relief against its *enforcement*. [The] majority recognizes that the President can seek relief from enforcement, but it does not vacate and remand for the lower courts to address this question. I would do so and instruct them to apply the standard articulated by Chief Justice Marshall in *Burr*: If the President is unable to comply because of his official duties, then he is entitled to injunctive and declaratory relief."

ALITO, J., also dissented, emphasizing that the President was effectively a target of the investigation. "In *McCulloch v. Maryland* [Ch. 2, Sec. 1], Maryland's sovereign taxing power had to yield, and in a similar way, a State's sovereign power to enforce its criminal laws must accommodate the indispensable role that the Constitution assigns to the Presidency. This must be the rule with respect to a state prosecution of a sitting President. Both the structure of the Government established by the Constitution and the Constitution's provisions on the impeachment and removal of a President make it clear that the prosecution of a sitting President is out of the question.

"If a sitting President were charged in New York County, would he be arrested and fingerprinted? He would presumably be required to appear for arraignment in criminal court, where the judge would set the conditions for his release. Could he be sent to Rikers Island or be required to post bail? Could the judge impose restrictions on his travel? If the President were scheduled to travel abroad—perhaps to attend a G-7 meeting—would he have to get judicial approval? [The] law applies equally to all persons, including a person who happens for a period of time to occupy the Presidency. But there is no question that the nature of the office demands in some instances that the application of laws be adjusted at least until the person's term in office ends.

"I agree with the Court that not all [subpoenas to the President] should be barred. There may be situations in which there is an urgent and critical need for the subpoenaed information. The situation in the Burr trial, where the documents at issue were sought by a criminal defendant to defend against a charge of treason, is a good example. But in a case like the one at hand, a subpoena should not be allowed unless a heightened standard is met."

(c)   TRUMP v. MAZARS USA, LLP, 140 S.Ct. 2019 (2020), was decided the same day as *Trump v. Vance*. ROBERTS, C.J., again wrote for the Court: "[T]hree committees of the U.S. House of Representatives issued four subpoenas seeking information about the finances of President Donald J. Trump, his children, and affiliated businesses. We have held that the House has authority under the Constitution to issue subpoenas to assist it in carrying out its legislative responsibilities. The House asserts that the financial information sought here—encompassing a decade's worth of transactions by the President and his family—will help guide legislative reform in areas ranging from money laundering and terrorism to foreign involvement in U.S. elections. The President contends that the House lacked a valid legislative aim and instead sought these records to harass him, expose personal matters, and conduct law enforcement activities beyond its authority.

"[The] President's information is sought not by prosecutors or private parties in connection with a particular judicial proceeding, but by committees of Congress that have set forth broad legislative objectives. Congress and the President—the two political branches established by the Constitution—have an ongoing relationship that the Framers intended to feature both rivalry and reciprocity. [Historically], disputes over congressional demands for presidential documents have not ended up in court. Instead, they have been hashed out [politically]." Chief Justice Roberts then described negotiations and compromises reached between Congress and Presidents Washington, Jefferson, Reagan, and Clinton.

"Quoting *Nixon*, the President asserts that the House must establish a 'demonstrated, specific need' for the financial information, just as the Watergate special prosecutor was required to do in order to obtain the tapes. And drawing on *Senate Select Committee on Presidential Campaign Activities v. Nixon*, 498 F.2d 725 (1974)—the D.C. Circuit case refusing to enforce the Senate subpoena for the tapes—the President and the Solicitor General argue that the House must show that the financial information is 'demonstrably critical' to its legislative purpose. We disagree that these demanding standards apply here. Unlike the cases before us, *Nixon* and *Senate Select Committee* involved Oval Office communications over which the President asserted executive privilege. That privilege safeguards the public interest in candid, confidential deliberations within the Executive Branch. [The] standards proposed by the President and the Solicitor General—if applied outside the context of privileged information—would risk seriously impeding Congress in carrying out its responsibilities. The President and the Solicitor General would apply the same exacting standards to *all* subpoenas for the President's information, without recognizing distinctions between privileged and nonprivileged information, between official and personal information, or between various legislative objectives. Such a categorical approach would represent a significant departure from the longstanding way of doing business between the branches, giving short shrift to Congress's important interests in conducting inquiries to obtain the information it needs to legislate effectively.

"[The] House meanwhile would have us ignore that these suits involve the President. Invoking our precedents concerning investigations that did not target the President's papers, the House urges us to uphold its subpoenas because they relate to a valid legislative purpose or concern a subject on which legislation could be had [citations and internal quotation marks omitted]. Far from accounting for separation of powers concerns, the House's approach aggravates them by leaving essentially no limits on the congressional power to subpoena the President's personal records. Any personal paper possessed by a President could potentially 'relate to' a conceivable subject of legislation, for Congress has broad legislative powers that touch a vast number of subjects. The President's financial records could relate to economic reform, medical records to health reform, school transcripts to education reform, and so on. Indeed, at argument, the House was unable to identify *any* type of information that lacks some relation to potential legislation.

"[Congressional] subpoenas for the President's personal information implicate weighty concerns regarding the separation of powers. Neither side, however, identifies an approach that accounts for these concerns. [A] balanced approach is necessary. [First,] courts should carefully assess whether the asserted legislative purpose warrants the significant step of involving the President and his papers. [Congress] may not rely on the President's information if other sources could reasonably provide Congress the information it needs in light of its particular legislative objective. [Second], to narrow the scope of possible conflict between the branches, courts should insist on a subpoena no broader than reasonably necessary to support Congress's legislative objective. [Third], courts should be attentive to the nature of the evidence offered by Congress to establish that a subpoena advances a valid legislative purpose. The more detailed and substantial the evidence of Congress's legislative purpose, the better. [Fourth], courts should be careful to assess the burdens imposed on the President by a subpoena. [Other] considerations may be pertinent as well; one case every two centuries does not afford enough experience for an exhaustive list." The Court remanded for application of the foregoing criteria.

THOMAS, J., dissented: "I would hold that Congress has no power to issue a legislative subpoena for private, nonofficial documents—whether they belong to the President or not. Congress may be able to obtain these documents as part of an investigation of the President, but to do so, it must proceed under the impeachment power."

ALITO, J., also dissented. Although he assumed *arguendo* that Congress may issue a subpoena to the President in the exercise of its legislative powers in some circumstances, he thought the Court's conditions were too permissive. He contended that "the House should provide a description of the type of legislation being considered, and while great specificity is not necessary, the description should be sufficient to permit a court to assess whether the particular records sought are of any special importance. The House should also spell out its constitutional authority to enact the type of legislation that it is contemplating, and it should justify the scope of the subpoenas in relation to the articulated legislative needs. In addition, it should explain why the subpoenaed information, as opposed to information available from other sources, is needed. Unless the House is required to make a showing along these lines, I would hold that enforcement of the subpoenas cannot be ordered."

4.   IMPEACHMENT OF THE PRESIDENT

P. 268, replace the introductory paragraph to Section 4 with the following:

In December 2019, for the third time in U.S. history, the House of Representatives impeached the President, who was then tried by the Senate. In January 2021, with just days remaining in his Term, President Donald Trump was impeached a second time. In each instance—Andrew Johnson in 1868, William Clinton in 1999, and Trump in 2020 and again in 2021—the Senate voted to acquit. A fourth President, Richard Nixon, would almost certainly have been impeached and very likely convicted and removed had he not resigned in 1974. In *Nixon v. United States* Ch. 1, Sec. 2 *supra,* (which concerned a federal judge with the same surname as the former President) the Supreme Court ruled that matters respecting congressional impeachments present nonjusticiable political questions. Thus, no judicial opinions address any of the important constitutional questions that may arise. The following notes consider some of these:

P. 271, add the following at the end of the chapter:

4.   ***Disqualification of former officers.*** One week before President Trump was scheduled to leave office, the House of Representatives impeached him for "incitement of insurrection" by encouraging his supporters to storm the Capitol while Congress was engaged in the ordinarily ceremonial function of counting Electoral College votes. The Senate trial did not occur until February 2021, after a new President had been inaugurated. Relying on various early precedents, including the

British Parliament's impeachment of Warren Hastings two years after his resignation as Governor General of Bengal, House managers argued that former officials remain subject to impeachment. Conviction, they said, was necessary to disqualify Trump from holding future federal office, including the Presidency. Many of the Senators who voted to acquit argued that disqualification can be an incident of conviction but that a former President cannot be tried on impeachment charges, which are available only for sitting officers. Does the text of the Constitution speak clearly to the permissibility of impeaching former officers? If the Senate had convicted and disqualified President Trump from future office holding but he nonetheless ran for President again, what person or body would have responsibility for determining his eligibility? Recall that *Nixon v. United States* [Ch. 1, Sec. 2] holds that a challenge to a judgment of impeachment presents a non-justiciable political question, placing special reliance on the difficulties that would ensue were a Presidential impeachment subject to judicial review. In light of *Nixon*, can courts hear a case seeking to *enforce* a Senate judgment of ineligibility following impeachment?

CHAPTER 4

STATE POWER TO REGULATE

■ ■ ■

2. BASIC DOCTRINAL PRINCIPLES AND THEIR APPLICATION

I. STATUTES THAT DISCRIMINATE ON THEIR FACES AGAINST INTERSTATE COMMERCE

P. 289, before *Maine v. Taylor*:

TENNESSEE WINE AND SPIRITS RETAILERS ASS'N v. TENNESSEE ALCOHOLIC BEVERAGE COMM'N, 139 S.Ct. 2449 (2019), invalidated a Tennessee statute that imposed a two-year duration-of-residency requirement for licenses to own and operate liquor stores. Writing for a 7–2 majority, ALITO, J., began by noting recent criticisms of dormant Commerce Clause doctrine, but he responded by citing original historical expectations that the Constitution would provide "protection against a broad swathe of state protectionist measures." Within the existing doctrinal framework, Tennessee's principal defense of its discriminatory residency test rested on § 2 of the Twenty-first Amendment, which provides that "[t]he transportation or importation into any State, Territory, or possession of the United States for delivery or use therein of intoxicating liquors, in violation of the laws thereof, is hereby prohibited." Despite some early judicial suggestions that § 2 gave the states plenary control over all matters involving alcohol, the Court had subsequently recognized that it must "scrutinize state alcohol laws for compliance with many constitutional provisions," including the First and Fourteenth Amendments. With respect to the dormant Commerce Clause, examination of relevant history "convince[s] us that the aim of § 2 was not to give states a free hand to restrict the importation of alcohol." GORSUCH, J., joined by Thomas, J., dissented: "[T]hose who ratified the [Twenty-first] Amendment wanted the States to be able to regulate the sale of liquor free of judicial meddling under the dormant Commerce Clause."

IV. STATUTES THAT DO NOT DISCRIMINATE ON THEIR FACES BUT NEVERTHELESS BURDEN INTERSTATE COMMERCE

P. 315, at the end of note 4:

5. *Abortion regulation.* Would legislation enacted by one state that forbade its citizens to procure abortions in another state, or that forbade doctors in other states to perform abortions on its citizens (or prescribe drugs to bring about the termination of their pregnancies), constitute extra-territorial legislation that is forbidden by the dormant Commerce Clause or other provisions of the Constitution? For discussion, see Richard H. Fallon, Jr., *If* Roe *Were Overruled: Abortion and the Constitution in a Post-*Roe *World,* 51 St. Louis U. L.J. 611, 626–640 (2007) (asserting that a state statute prohibiting citizens from obtaining abortions anywhere would not discriminate against interstate commerce but noting complexities under the underdeveloped doctrinal strand involving extraterritorial regulation).

CHAPTER 5

SUBSTANTIVE PROTECTION OF ECONOMIC INTERESTS

■ ■ ■

4. OTHER LIMITS ON ECONOMIC LEGISLATION: THE PROHIBITION AGAINST "TAKING" "PRIVATE PROPERTY" WITHOUT JUST COMPENSATION

P. 398, replace the first two paragraphs (on *Horne*) with:

In CEDAR POINT NURSERY v. HASID, 141 S.Ct. 2063 (2021), ROBERTS, C.J., wrote for the Court that a California regulation granting union organizers access to private agricultural property "for up to three hours per day, 120 days per year" was a physical invasion subject to *Loretto*'s *per se* rule: "Government action that physically appropriates property is no less a physical taking because it arises from a regulation. [The] essential question [is] whether the government has physically taken property for itself or someone else—by whatever means—or has instead restricted a property owner's ability to use his own property. Whenever a regulation results in a physical appropriation of property, a *per se* taking has occurred, and *Penn Central* has no place. [The] regulation grants union organizers a right to physically enter and occupy the growers' land for three hours per day, 120 days per year. Rather than restraining the growers' use of their own property, the regulation appropriates for the enjoyment of third parties the owners' right to exclude. [The] duration of an appropriation—just like the size of an appropriation, see *Loretto*,—bears only on the amount of compensation."

BREYER, J., joined by Sotomayor and Kagan, JJ., dissented on the ground that the "regulation does not 'appropriate' anything; it regulates the employers' right to exclude others. [The] 'access' that it grants union organizers does not amount to any traditional property interest in land. [It] gives union organizers the right temporarily to invade a portion of the property owners' land. It thereby limits the landowners' right to exclude certain others. The regulation *regulates* (but does not *appropriate*) the owners' right to exclude." Thus, according to the dissent, the majority had disregarded *Loretto*'s distinction between "permanent physical occupations" and "temporary limitations on the right to exclude."

29

CHAPTER 6

PROTECTION OF INDIVIDUAL RIGHTS: DUE PROCESS, THE BILL OF RIGHTS, AND UNENUMERATED RIGHTS

■ ■ ■

1. APPLICABILITY OF THE BILL OF RIGHTS TO THE STATES; NATURE AND SCOPE OF FOURTEENTH AMENDMENT DUE PROCESS

II. IS THE BILL OF RIGHTS INCORPORATED "JOT-FOR-JOT"?

Pp. 418–20, delete the note on *Baldwin*, *Williams*, **and** *Apodaca*.

III. IN *MCDONALD V. CITY OF CHICAGO*, THE COURT LOOKS BACK ON ITS "INCORPORATION" OF BILL OF RIGHTS GUARANTEES

P. 421, delete footnote 14 and insert immediately before IV:

In TIMBS v. INDIANA, 139 S.Ct. 682 (2019), GINSBURG, J., wrote for the Court that "the historical and logical case for concluding that the Fourteenth Amendment incorporates the Excessive Fines Clause is overwhelming." The Court rejected the State's contention that the Fourteenth Amendment did not incorporate the Clause's application to civil *in rem* forfeitures that are at least partly punitive. The decision was unanimous in result, but THOMAS, J., concurred only in the judgment. Adhering to a view he expressed in *McDonald* (Sec. 7 *infra*), he would have relied on the Fourteenth Amendment's Privileges or Immunities Clause as the basis for incorporation. Concurring in the majority opinion, GORSUCH, J., "acknowledge[d]" that "[a]s an original matter . . . the appropriate vehicle for incorporation may well be the Fourteenth Amendment's Privileges or Immunities Clause, rather than, as this Court has long assumed, the Due Process Clause." However, he continued, "nothing in this case turns on that question, and, regardless of the precise vehicle, there can be no serious doubt that the Fourteenth Amendment requires the States to respect the freedom from excessive fines enshrined in the Eighth Amendment."

RAMOS v. LOUISIANA, 140 S.Ct. 1390 (2020), presented the question whether the Sixth Amendment requirement of a unanimous twelve-person jury in serious criminal cases is incorporated. GORSUCH, J., wrote for the Court: "In 48 States and federal court, a single juror's vote to acquit is enough to prevent a conviction. But not in Louisiana. Along with Oregon, Louisiana has long punished people based on 10-to-2 verdicts. [Wherever] we might look to determine what the term 'trial by an impartial jury trial' meant at the time of the Sixth Amendment's adoption—whether it's the common law, state practices in the founding era, or opinions and treatises written soon afterward—the answer is unmistakable. A jury must reach a unanimous verdict in order to convict.

"There can be no question either that the Sixth Amendment's unanimity requirement applies to state and federal criminal trials equally. This Court has long explained that the Sixth Amendment right to a jury trial is 'fundamental to the American scheme of justice' and incorporated against the States under the Fourteenth Amendment. This Court has long explained, too, that incorporated provisions of the Bill of Rights bear the same content when asserted against States as they do when asserted against the federal government. So if the Sixth Amendment's right to a jury trial requires a unanimous verdict to support a conviction in federal court, it requires no less in state court.

"How, despite these seemingly straightforward principles, have Louisiana's and Oregon's laws managed to hang on for so long? It turns out that the Sixth Amendment's otherwise simple story took a strange turn. [In] *Apodaca* v. *Oregon,* 406 U.S. 404 (1972), [four] dissenting Justices would not have hesitated to strike down the States' laws, recognizing that the Sixth Amendment requires unanimity and that this guarantee is fully applicable against the States under the Fourteenth Amendment. But a four-Justice plurality [declared] that the real question [was] whether unanimity serves an important 'function' in 'contemporary society.' [Justice] Powell agreed that, as a matter of 'history and precedent, the Sixth Amendment requires a unanimous jury verdict to convict.' But, on the other hand, he argued that the Fourteenth Amendment does not render this guarantee against the federal government fully applicable against the States. In this way, Justice Powell doubled down on his belief in 'dual-track' incorporation—the idea that a single right can mean two different things depending on whether it is being invoked against the federal or a state government.

"[Even] if we accepted the premise that *Apodaca* established a precedent, no one on the Court today is prepared to say it was rightly decided, and *stare decisis* isn't supposed to be the art of methodically ignoring what everyone knows to be true. [Louisiana and Oregon] credibly claim that the number of nonunanimous felony convictions still on direct appeal are somewhere in the hundreds, and retrying or plea bargaining these cases will surely impose a cost. But new rules of criminal procedures usually do, often affecting significant numbers of pending cases across the whole country."

SOTOMAYOR and KAVANAUGH, JJ., each wrote a partial concurrence explaining their respective views of *stare decisis*. THOMAS, J., concurred in the judgment, reiterating his view that the Fourteenth Amendment's Privileges or Immunities Clause provides the proper basis for incorporation. *See McDonald, infra*, Sec. 7.

ALITO, J., joined by Roberts, C.J., and Kagan, J., dissented on *stare decisis* grounds: The Court "imposes a potentially crushing burden on the courts and criminal justice systems of [Louisiana and Oregon]. Whatever one may think about the correctness of [*Apodaca*], it has elicited enormous and entirely reasonable reliance. And before this Court decided to intervene, the decision appeared to have little practical importance going forward. Louisiana has now abolished non-unanimous verdicts, and Oregon seemed on the verge of doing the same until the Court intervened."

IV. HOW MUCH MORE SPECIFIC ARE PROVISIONS OF THE BILL OF RIGHTS THAN DUE PROCESS GENERALLY? THE CASE OF BODILY EXTRACTIONS

P. 425, at the end of note 2:

3. *Mandatory vaccination.* As this Supplement went to press in summer 2021, three safe and effective vaccines for COVID-19 had received emergency use authorization and were widely available for free in the United States. However, some vulnerable people are unable to receive the vaccine due to underlying medical conditions. Nonetheless, unvaccinated individuals can be protected by a vaccine administered to others through *herd immunity*: when a sufficiently high proportion of the community has been vaccinated or acquired immunity from the disease itself, the contagion ceases to spread because it does not encounter sufficiently many vulnerable hosts. The portion of the population that must be vaccinated for a community to achieve herd immunity depends on the vaccine's effectiveness and the disease's contagiousness. Given that substantial numbers of Americans without any underlying medical condition have declined to be vaccinated, herd immunity against COVID-19 might not be achieved. Even if it is, herd immunity might be unachievable against other deadly diseases without a government vaccination mandate. Would such a mandate violate a right to bodily autonomy?

JACOBSON v. MASSACHUSETTS, 197 U.S. 11 (1905), per HARLAN, J., upheld a criminal conviction of the defendant for refusal to submit to a free state-mandated vaccination against smallpox: The defendant relied on "the general theory of those of the medical profession who attach little or no value to vaccination as a means of preventing the spread of smallpox, or who think that vaccination causes other diseases of the body. What everybody knows, the court must know, and therefore the state court judicially knew, as this court knows, that an opposite theory accords with the common belief and is maintained by high medical authority. We must assume that, when the statute in question was passed, the legislature of Massachusetts was not unaware of these opposing theories, and was compelled, of necessity, to choose between them. [The] state legislature proceeded upon the theory which recognized vaccination as at least an effective, if not the best, known way in which to meet and suppress the evils of a smallpox epidemic that imperiled an entire population. [Whatever] may be thought of the expediency of this statute, it cannot be affirmed to be, beyond question, in palpable conflict with the Constitution. Nor, in view of the methods employed to stamp out the disease of smallpox, can anyone confidently assert that the means prescribed by the State to that end has no real or substantial relation to the protection of the public health and the public safety."

Note that *Jacobson* was decided in the same year as *Lochner*, whose author, Peckham, J., along with Brewer, J., dissented without opinion. Does *Jacobson* apply the same test as modern bodily autonomy cases? If not, is it nonetheless still good law?

2.   REPRODUCTIVE FREEDOM

Introductory Note on the Right of "Privacy"

P. 442, at the end of footnote 14:

McCorvey's story took one final surprise turn. Before her death in February 2017, she issued what she sardonically called a "deathbed confession" that she was never really pro-life after all. Footage was included in a television documentary that premiered on the FX Network in 2020. *AKA Jane Roe* also showed financial records indicating that McCorvey had been paid nearly half a million dollars by pro-life organizations and individuals.

Pp. 455–57, after note 4, delete notes on Abortion Funding and Private Insurance

Pp. 470–84, replace notes and cases with the following principal case and notes:

The Court Overturns *Roe* and *Casey*

DOBBS V. JACKSON WOMEN'S HEALTH ORG.
___ U.S. ___, 142 S.Ct. 2228, ___ L.Ed.2d ___ (2022).

JUSTICE ALITO delivered the opinion of the Court.

Abortion presents a profound moral issue on which Americans hold sharply conflicting views. Some believe fervently that a human person comes into being at conception and that abortion ends an innocent life.

Others feel just as strongly that any regulation of abortion invades a woman's right to control her own body and prevents women from achieving full equality. Still others in a third group think that abortion should be allowed under some but not all circumstances, and those within this group hold a variety of views about the particular restrictions that should be imposed.

[Before] us now is [a Mississippi] law that generally prohibits an abortion after the 15th week of pregnancy—several weeks before the point at which a fetus is now regarded as "viable" outside the womb. In defending this law, the State's primary argument is that we should reconsider and overrule *Roe* and *Casey* and once again allow each State to regulate abortion as its citizens wish.

We hold that *Roe* and *Casey* must be overruled. The Constitution makes no reference to abortion, and no such right is implicitly protected by any constitutional provision, including the one on which the defenders of *Roe* and *Casey* now chiefly rely—the Due Process Clause of the Fourteenth Amendment. That provision has been held to guarantee some rights that are not mentioned in the Constitution, but any such right must be "deeply rooted in this Nation's history and tradition" and "implicit in the concept of ordered liberty." *Washington* v. *Glucksberg* [Sec. 3, infra]. The right to abortion does not fall within this category. Until the latter part of the 20th century, such a right was entirely unknown in American law. Indeed, when the Fourteenth Amendment was adopted, three quarters of the States made abortion a crime at all stages of pregnancy. The abortion right is also critically different from any other right that this Court has held to fall within the Fourteenth Amendment's protection of "liberty." *Roe*'s defenders characterize the abortion right as similar to the rights recognized in past decisions involving matters such as intimate sexual relations, contraception, and marriage, but abortion is fundamentally different, as both *Roe* and *Casey* acknowledged, because it destroys what those decisions called "fetal life" and what the law now before us describes as an "unborn human being."

Stare decisis, the doctrine on which *Casey*'s controlling opinion was based, does not compel unending adherence to *Roe*'s abuse of judicial authority. *Roe* was egregiously wrong from the start. Its reasoning was exceptionally weak, and the decision has had damaging consequences. And far from bringing about a national settlement of the abortion issue, *Roe* and *Casey* have enflamed debate and deepened division. It is time to heed the Constitution and return the issue of abortion to the people's elected representatives.

[*Roe*] was remarkably loose in its treatment of the constitutional text. It held that the abortion right, which is not mentioned in the Constitution, is part of a right to privacy, which is also not mentioned. And that privacy right, *Roe* observed, had been found to spring from no fewer than five different constitutional provisions—the First, Fourth, Fifth, Ninth, and Fourteenth Amendments. *Roe* expressed the "feel[ing]" that the Fourteenth Amendment was the provision that did the work, but its message seemed to be that the abortion right could be found *somewhere* in the Constitution and that specifying its exact location was not of paramount importance. The *Casey* Court did not defend this unfocused analysis and instead grounded its decision solely on the theory that the right to obtain an abortion is part of the "liberty" protected by the Fourteenth Amendment's Due Process Clause.

We discuss [due process] below, but before doing so, we briefly address one additional constitutional provision that some of respondents' *amici* have now offered as yet another potential home for the abortion right: the Fourteenth Amendment's Equal Protection Clause. Neither *Roe* nor *Casey* saw fit to invoke this theory, and it is squarely foreclosed by our precedents, which establish that a State's regulation of abortion is not a sex-based classification and is thus not subject to the "heightened scrutiny" that applies to such classifications. The regulation of a medical procedure that only one sex can undergo does not trigger heightened constitutional scrutiny unless the regulation is a "mere pretex[t] designed to effect an invidious discrimination against members of one sex or the other." *Geduldig v. Aiello* [Ch. 9, Sec. 3, II, infra]. And as the Court has stated, the "goal of preventing abortion" does not constitute "invidiously discriminatory animus" against women. *Bray v. Alexandria Women's Health Clinic* [Ch. 11, Sec. 2, I, infra]. Accordingly, laws regulating or prohibiting abortion are not subject to heightened scrutiny. Rather, they are governed by the same standard of review as other health and safety measures.

[Substantive due process] has long been controversial. But our decisions have held that the Due Process Clause protects two categories of substantive rights. The first consists of rights guaranteed by the first eight Amendments. [This] Court has held that the Due Process Clause of the Fourteenth Amendment "incorporates" the great majority of those rights and thus makes them equally applicable to the States. The second category—which is the one in question here—comprises a select list of fundamental rights that are not mentioned anywhere in the Constitution. In deciding whether a right falls into either of these categories, the Court has long asked whether the right is "deeply rooted in [our] history and tradition" and whether it is essential to our Nation's "scheme of ordered liberty." *Timbs*. And in conducting this inquiry, we have engaged in a careful analysis of the history of the right at issue. *Timbs* and *McDonald v. City of Chicago* [Sec. 7, infra] concerned the question whether the Fourteenth Amendment protects rights that are expressly set out in the Bill of Rights, and it would be anomalous if similar historical support were not required when a putative right is not mentioned anywhere in the Constitution.

In interpreting what is meant by the Fourteenth Amendment's reference to "liberty," we must guard against the natural human tendency to confuse what that Amendment protects with our own ardent views about the liberty that Americans should enjoy. [On] occasion, [the] Court [has] fallen into the freewheeling judicial policymaking that characterized discredited decisions such as *Lochner*. The Court must not fall prey to such an unprincipled approach. Instead, guided by the history and tradition that map the essential components of our Nation's concept of ordered liberty, we must ask what the *Fourteenth Amendment* means by the term "liberty."

Until the latter part of the 20th century, there was no support in American law for a constitutional right to obtain an abortion. No state constitutional provision had recognized such a right. Until a few years before *Roe* was handed down, no federal or state court had recognized such a right. [Not] only was there no support for such a constitutional right until shortly before *Roe*, but abortion had long been a *crime* in every single State. At common law, abortion was criminal in at least some stages of pregnancy and was regarded as unlawful and could have very serious consequences at all stages. American law followed the common law until a wave of statutory restrictions in the 1800s expanded criminal liability for abortions. By the time of the adoption of the Fourteenth Amendment, three-quarters of the States had made abortion a crime at any stage of pregnancy, and the remaining States would soon follow. *Roe* either ignored or misstated this history, and *Casey* declined to reconsider *Roe*'s faulty historical analysis. It is therefore important to set the record straight.

[Under the common law], abortion was a crime at least after "quickening"—*i.e.*, the first felt movement of the fetus in the womb, which usually occurs between the 16th and 18th week of pregnancy. [Henry] de Bracton's 13th-century treatise explained that if a person has "struck a pregnant woman, or has given her poison, whereby he has caused abortion, if the foetus be already formed and animated, and particularly if it be animated, he commits homicide." 2 De Legibus et Consuetudinibus Angliae 279 (T. Twiss ed. 1879). Sir Edward Coke's 17th-century treatise likewise asserted that abortion of a quick child was "murder" if the "childe be born alive" and a "great misprision" if the "childe dieth in her body." 3 Institutes of the Laws of England 50–51 (1644). [Two] treatises by Sir Matthew Hale likewise described abortion of a quick child who died in the womb as a "great crime" and a "great misprision." Pleas of the Crown 53 (P. Glazebrook ed. 1972); 1 History of the Pleas of the Crown 433 (1736) (Hale). And writing near the time of the adoption of our Constitution, William Blackstone explained that abortion of a "quick" child was "by the ancient law homicide or manslaughter" (citing Bracton), and at least a very "heinous misdemeanor" (citing Coke). 1 Commentaries on the Laws of

England 129–130 (7th ed. 1775) (Blackstone). English cases dating all the way back to the 13th century corroborate the treatises' statements that abortion was a crime. Although a pre-quickening abortion was not itself considered homicide, it does not follow that abortion was *permissible* at common law. [Quite] to the contrary, [in a] 1732 case, [the] judge said of the charge of abortion (with no mention of quickening) that he had "never met with a case so barbarous and unnatural." Similarly, an indictment from 1602, which did not distinguish between a pre-quickening and post-quickening abortion, described abortion as "pernicious" and "against the peace of our Lady the Queen, her crown and dignity."

[Hale] wrote that if a physician gave a woman "with child" a "potion" to cause an abortion, and the woman died, it was "murder" because the potion was given *"unlawfully* to destroy her child within her." 1 Hale 429–430 (emphasis added). As Blackstone explained, to be "murder" a killing had to be done with "malice aforethought, . . . either express or implied." 4 Blackstone 198 (emphasis deleted). In the case of an abortionist, Blackstone wrote, "the law will imply [malice]" for the same reason that it would imply malice if a person who intended to kill one person accidentally killed a different person. [In] sum, although common-law authorities differed on the severity of punishment for abortions committed at different points in pregnancy, none endorsed the practice. Moreover, we are aware of no common-law case or authority, and the parties have not pointed to any, that remotely suggests a positive *right* to procure an abortion at any stage of pregnancy.

In this country, the historical record is similar. [Manuals] for justices of the peace printed in the Colonies in the 18th century typically restated the common-law rule on abortion, and some manuals repeated Hale's and Blackstone's statements that anyone who prescribed medication "unlawfully to destroy the child" would be guilty of murder if the woman died. [The] few cases available from the early colonial period corroborate that abortion was a crime. In Maryland in 1652, for example, an indictment charged that a man "Murtherously endeavoured to destroy or Murther the Child by him begotten in the Womb." *Proprietary* v. *Mitchell*, 10 Md. Archives 80 (1652) (W. Browne ed. 1891). And by the 19th century, courts frequently explained that the common law made abortion of a quick child a crime. [Citations omitted].

[The] quickening rule [was] abandoned in the 19th century. [In] 1803, the British Parliament made abortion a crime at all stages of pregnancy and authorized the imposition of severe punishment. [In] this country during the 19th century, the vast majority of the States enacted statutes criminalizing abortion at all stages of pregnancy. By 1868, the year when the Fourteenth Amendment was ratified, three-quarters of the States, 28 out of 37, had enacted statutes making abortion a crime even if it was performed before quickening. Of the nine States that had not yet criminalized abortion at all stages, all but one did so by 1910. [The] trend in the Territories that would become the last 13 States was similar: All of them criminalized abortion at all stages of pregnancy between 1850 (the Kingdom of Hawaii) and 1919 (New Mexico). This overwhelming consensus endured until the day *Roe* was decided. [The] inescapable conclusion is that a right to abortion is not deeply rooted in the Nation's history and traditions. Not only are respondents and their *amici* unable to show that a constitutional right to abortion was established when the Fourteenth Amendment was adopted, but they have found no support for the existence of an abortion right that predates the latter part of the 20th century.

[Instead] of seriously pressing the argument that the abortion right itself has deep roots, supporters of *Roe* and *Casey* contend that the abortion right is an integral part of a broader entrenched right. *Roe* termed this a right to privacy and *Casey* described it as the freedom to make "intimate and personal choices" that are "central to personal dignity and autonomy." *Casey* elaborated: "At the heart of liberty is the right to define one's own concept of existence, of meaning, of the universe, and of the mystery of human life." The Court did not claim that this broadly framed right is absolute, and no such claim would be plausible. While individuals are certainly free *to think* and *to say* what they wish about "existence," "meaning," the "universe," and "the mystery of human life," they are not always free *to act* in accordance with those thoughts. License to act on the basis of such beliefs may correspond to one of the many understandings of "liberty," but it is certainly not "ordered liberty."

Nor does the right to obtain an abortion have a sound basis in precedent. *Casey* relied on cases involving the right to marry a person of a different race, *Loving v. Virginia* [Sec. 5, II, infra]; the right to marry while in prison, *Turner v. Safely* [Sec. 5, II, infra]; the right to obtain contraceptives, *Griswold, Eisenstadt, Carey*; the right to reside with relatives, *Moore v. East Cleveland* [Sec. 5, I, infra]; the right to make decisions about the education of one's children, *Pierce, Meyer*; the right not to be sterilized without consent, *Skinner*; and the right in certain circumstances not to undergo involuntary surgery, forced administration of drugs, or other substantially similar procedures, *Winston, Washington v. Harper* [Sec. 5, III, infra], *Rochin*. Respondents and the Solicitor General also rely on post-*Casey* decisions like *Lawrence v. Texas* [Sec. 4, infra] (right to engage in private, consensual sexual acts), and *Obergefell v. Hodges* [Sec. 5, II, infra] (right to marry a person of the same sex). These attempts to justify abortion through appeals to a broader right to autonomy and to define one's "concept of existence" prove too much. Those criteria, at a high level of generality, could license fundamental rights to illicit drug use, prostitution, and the like. None of these rights has any claim to being deeply rooted in history.

What sharply distinguishes the abortion right from the rights recognized in the cases on which *Roe* and *Casey* rely is something that both those decisions acknowledged: Abortion destroys what those decisions call "potential life" and what the law at issue in this case regards as the life of an "unborn human being." [None] of the other decisions cited by *Roe* and *Casey* involved the critical moral question posed by abortion. They are therefore inapposite. They do not support the right to obtain an abortion, and by the same token, our conclusion that the Constitution does not confer such a right does not undermine them in any way.

[Defenders] of *Roe* and *Casey* do not claim that any new scientific learning calls for a different answer to the underlying moral question, but they do contend that changes in society require the recognition of a constitutional right to obtain an abortion. Without the availability of abortion, they maintain, people will be inhibited from exercising their freedom to choose the types of relationships they desire, and women will be unable to compete with men in the workplace and in other endeavors. Americans who believe that abortion should be restricted press countervailing arguments about modern developments. They note that attitudes about the pregnancy of unmarried women have changed drastically; that federal and state laws ban discrimination on the basis of pregnancy; that leave for pregnancy and childbirth are now guaranteed by law in many cases; that the costs of medical care associated with pregnancy are covered by insurance or government assistance; that States have increasingly adopted "safe haven" laws, which generally allow women to drop off babies anonymously; and that a woman who puts her newborn up for adoption today has little reason to fear that the baby will not find a suitable home. They also claim that many people now have a new appreciation of fetal life and that when prospective parents who want to have a child view a sonogram, they typically have no doubt that what they see is their daughter or son. Both sides make important policy arguments, but supporters of *Roe* and *Casey* must show that this Court has the authority to weigh those arguments and decide how abortion may be regulated in the States. They have failed to make that showing, and we thus return the power to weigh those arguments to the people and their elected representatives.

[The] most striking feature of the dissent is the absence of any serious discussion of the legitimacy of the States' interest in protecting fetal life. This is evident in the analogy that the dissent draws between the abortion right and the rights recognized in *Griswold* (contraception), *Eisenstadt* (same), *Lawrence* (sexual conduct with member of the same sex), and *Obergefell* (same-sex marriage). Perhaps this is designed to stoke unfounded fear that our decision will imperil those other rights, but the dissent's analogy is objectionable for a more important reason: what it reveals about the dissent's views on the protection of what *Roe* called "potential life." The exercise of the rights at issue in *Griswold*, *Eisenstadt*, *Lawrence*, and *Obergefell* does not destroy a "potential life," but an abortion has that effect. So if the rights at issue in those cases are fundamentally the same as the right recognized in *Roe* and *Casey*, the implication is clear: The Constitution does not permit the States to regard the destruction of a "potential life" as a matter of any significance.

[Our] opinion is not based on any view about if and when prenatal life is entitled to any of the rights enjoyed after birth. The dissent, by contrast, would impose on the people a particular theory about when the rights of personhood begin. According to the dissent, the Constitution *requires* the States to regard a fetus as lacking even the most basic human right—to live—at least until an arbitrary point in a pregnancy has passed. Nothing in the Constitution or in our Nation's legal traditions authorizes the Court to adopt that " 'theory of life.' "

[*Stare decisis*] is "not an inexorable command" and it "is at its weakest when we interpret the Constitution." [Citations omitted.] An erroneous constitutional decision can be fixed by amending the Constitution, but our Constitution is notoriously hard to amend. Therefore, in appropriate circumstances we must be willing to reconsider and, if necessary, overrule constitutional decisions.

Some of our most important constitutional decisions have overruled prior precedents. We mention three. In *Brown v. Board of Education*, the Court repudiated the "separate but equal" doctrine, which had allowed States to maintain racially segregated schools and other facilities. In so doing, the Court overruled the infamous decision in *Plessy v. Ferguson* along with six other Supreme Court precedents that had applied the separate-but-equal rule. In *West Coast Hotel*, the Court overruled *Adkins*, which had held that a law setting minimum wages for women violated the "liberty" protected by the Fifth Amendment's Due Process Clause. *West Coast Hotel* signaled the demise of an entire line of important precedents that had protected an individual liberty right against state and federal health and welfare legislation. Finally, in *West Virginia Bd. of Ed. v. Barnette* [Ch. 7, Sec. 9, I, *infra*], after the lapse of only three years, the Court overruled *Minersville School Dist. v. Gobitis*, 310 U.S. 586 (1940), and held that public school students could not be compelled to salute the flag in violation of their sincere beliefs. *Barnette* stands out because nothing had changed during the intervening period other than the Court's belated recognition that its earlier decision had been seriously wrong. On many other occasions, this Court has overruled important constitutional decisions.[48] Without these decisions, American constitutional law as we know it would be unrecognizable, and this would be a different country.

---

[48]　[Ct's Note] [The Court listed 28 decisions and the precedents they respectively overruled.]

[Five] factors weigh strongly in favor of overruling *Roe* and *Casey*: the nature of their error, the quality of their reasoning, the "workability" of the rules they imposed on the country, their disruptive effect on other areas of the law, and the absence of concrete reliance.

The nature of the Court's error. [*Roe* was] egregiously wrong and deeply damaging. [*Casey*] described itself as calling both sides of the national controversy to resolve their debate, but in doing so, *Casey* necessarily declared a winning side. Those on the losing side—those who sought to advance the State's interest in fetal life—could no longer seek to persuade their elected representatives to adopt policies consistent with their views. The Court short-circuited the democratic process by closing it to the large number of Americans who dissented in any respect from *Roe*. * * *

The quality of the reasoning. [*Roe's*] elaborate scheme was the Court's own brainchild. Neither party advocated the trimester framework; nor did either party or any *amicus* argue that "viability" should mark the point at which the scope of the abortion right and a State's regulatory authority should be substantially transformed. [Citing] a broad array of cases, the Court found support for a constitutional "right of personal privacy," but it conflated two very different meanings of the term: the right to shield information from disclosure and the right to make and implement important personal decisions without governmental interference. Only the cases involving this second sense of the term could have any possible relevance to the abortion issue, and some of the cases in that category involved personal decisions that were obviously very, very far afield. See *Pierce*; *Meyer*. What remained was a handful of cases having something to do with marriage [or] procreation. [But] none of these decisions involved what is distinctive about abortion: its effect on what *Roe* termed "potential life."

[What] *Roe* did not provide was any cogent justification for the lines it drew. Why, for example, does a State have no authority to regulate first trimester abortions for the purpose of protecting a woman's health? The Court's only explanation was that mortality rates for abortion at that stage were lower than the mortality rates for childbirth. But the Court did not explain why mortality rates were the only factor that a State could legitimately consider. Many health and safety regulations aim to avoid adverse health consequences short of death. And the Court did not explain why it departed from the normal rule that courts defer to the judgments of legislatures "in areas fraught with medical and scientific uncertainties."

An even more glaring deficiency was *Roe's* failure to justify the critical distinction it drew between pre- and post-viability abortions. [The viability] line has not found much support among philosophers and ethicists who have attempted to justify a right to abortion. Some have argued that a fetus should not be entitled to legal protection until it acquires the characteristics that they regard as defining what it means to be a "person." Among the characteristics that have been offered as essential attributes of "personhood" are sentience, self-awareness, the ability to reason, or some combination thereof. By this logic, it would be an open question whether even born individuals, including young children or those afflicted with certain developmental or medical conditions, merit protection as "persons." But even if one takes the view that "personhood" begins when a certain attribute or combination of attributes is acquired, it is very hard to see why viability should mark the point where "personhood" begins. The most obvious problem with any such argument is that viability is heavily dependent on factors that have nothing to do with the characteristics of a fetus, [such as] the state of neonatal care at a particular point in time.

[When] *Casey* revisited *Roe* almost 20 years later, very little of *Roe*'s reasoning was defended or preserved. The Court [made] no real effort to remedy one of the greatest weaknesses in *Roe*'s analysis: its much-criticized discussion of viability. The Court retained what it called *Roe*'s "central holding"—that a State may not regulate pre-viability abortions for the purpose of protecting fetal life—but it provided no principled defense of the viability line. Instead, it merely rephrased what *Roe* had said, stating that viability marked the point at which "the independent existence of a second life can in reason and fairness be the object of state protection that now overrides the rights of the woman." Why "reason and fairness" demanded that the line be drawn at viability the Court did not explain. And the Justices who authored the controlling opinion [candidly] acknowledged "the reservations [some] of us may have in reaffirming [that] holding of *Roe*." * * *

Workability. Our precedents counsel that another important consideration in deciding whether a precedent should be overruled is whether the rule it imposes is workable—that is, whether it can be understood and applied in a consistent and predictable manner. [The *Casey*] "undue burden" test [asks] courts to examine a law's effect on women, but a regulation may have a very different impact on different women for a variety of reasons, including their places of residence, financial resources, family situations, work and personal obligations, knowledge about fetal development and abortion, psychological and emotional disposition and condition, and the firmness of their desire to obtain abortions. In order to determine whether a regulation presents a substantial obstacle to women, a court needs to know which set of women it should have in mind and how many of the women in this set must find that an obstacle is "substantial." *Casey* provided no clear answer to these questions.

The difficulty of applying *Casey*'s new rules surfaced in that very case [and] also produced disagreement in later cases. [It] has generated a long list of Circuit conflicts. [The] Courts of Appeals [have] disagreed on the legality of parental notification rules. They have disagreed about bans on certain dilation and evacuation procedures. They have disagreed about when an increase in the time needed to reach a clinic constitutes an undue burden. And they have disagreed on whether a State may regulate abortions performed because of the fetus's race, sex, or disability. [And] they have candidly outlined *Casey*'s many other problems. * * *

Effect on other areas of law. *Roe* and *Casey* have led to the distortion of many important but unrelated legal doctrines, and that effect provides further support for overruling those decisions. [The] Court's abortion cases have diluted the strict standard for facial constitutional challenges. [They] have ignored the Court's third-party standing doctrine. [T]hey have disregarded standard *res judicata* principles. They have flouted the ordinary rules on the severability of unconstitutional provisions, as well as the rule that statutes should be read where possible to avoid unconstitutionality. And they have distorted First Amendment doctrines. * * *

Reliance interests. [Unable] to find reliance in the conventional sense, the controlling opinion in *Casey* perceived a more intangible form of reliance. It wrote that "people [had] organized intimate relationships and made choices that define their views of themselves and their places in society . . . in reliance on the availability of abortion in the event that contraception should fail" and that "[t]he ability of women to participate equally in the economic and social life of the Nation has been facilitated by their ability to control their reproductive lives." [But] *Casey*'s notion of reliance [finds] little support in our cases. [When] a concrete reliance interest is asserted, courts are equipped to evaluate the claim, but assessing the novel and intangible form of reliance endorsed by the *Casey* plurality is another matter. That form of reliance depends on an empirical question that is hard for anyone—and in particular, for a court—to assess, namely, the effect of the abortion right on society and in particular on the lives of women.

[Unable] to show concrete reliance on *Roe* and *Casey* themselves, the Solicitor General suggests that overruling those decisions would "threaten the Court's precedents holding that the Due Process Clause protects other rights." Brief for United States (citing *Obergefell*; *Lawrence*; *Griswold*). That is not correct for reasons we have already discussed. As even the *Casey* plurality recognized, "[a]bortion is a unique act" because it terminates "life or potential life." [To] ensure that our decision is not misunderstood or mischaracterized, we emphasize that our decision concerns the constitutional right to abortion and no other right. Nothing in this opinion should be understood to cast doubt on precedents that do not concern abortion.

[Having] shown that traditional *stare decisis* factors do not weigh in favor of retaining *Roe* or *Casey*, we must address one final argument that featured prominently in the *Casey* plurality opinion. [The] *Casey* plurality was certainly right that it is important for the public to perceive that our decisions are based on principle, and we should make every effort to achieve that objective by issuing opinions that carefully show how a proper understanding of the law leads to the results we reach. But we cannot exceed the scope of our authority under the Constitution, and we cannot allow our decisions to be affected by any extraneous influences such as concern about the public's reaction to our work. [The] Court has no authority to decree that an erroneous precedent is *permanently* exempt from evaluation under traditional *stare decisis* principles. A precedent of this Court is subject to the usual principles of *stare decisis* under which adherence to precedent is the norm but not an inexorable command. If the rule were otherwise, erroneous decisions like *Plessy* and *Lochner* would still be the law. That is not how *stare decisis* operates.

The *Casey* plurality also misjudged the practical limits of this Court's influence. *Roe* certainly did not succeed in ending division on the issue of abortion. On the contrary, *Roe* "inflamed" a national issue that has remained bitterly divisive for the past half century. *Casey* (opinion of Scalia, J.); see also Ruth Bader Ginsburg, *Speaking in a Judicial Voice*, 67 N.Y.U.L.Rev. 1185 (1992) (*Roe* may have "halted a political process," "prolonged divisiveness," and "deferred stable settlement of the issue"). And for the past 30 years, *Casey* has done the same. Neither decision has ended debate over the issue of a constitutional right to obtain an abortion. [This] Court cannot bring about the permanent resolution of a rancorous national controversy simply by dictating a settlement and telling the people to move on. [We] therefore hold that the Constitution does not confer a right to abortion. *Roe* and *Casey* must be overruled, and the authority to regulate abortion must be returned to the people and their elected representatives.

[We] must now decide what standard will govern if state abortion regulations undergo constitutional challenge and whether the law before us satisfies the appropriate standard. [Under] our precedents, rational-basis review is the appropriate standard for such challenges. As we have explained, procuring an abortion is not a fundamental constitutional right because such a right has no basis in the Constitution's text or in our Nation's history. [A] law regulating abortion, like other health and welfare laws, is entitled to a "strong presumption of validity." It must be sustained if there is a rational basis on which the legislature could have thought that it would serve legitimate state interests. These legitimate interests include respect for and preservation of prenatal life at all stages of development; the protection of maternal health and safety; the elimination of particularly gruesome or barbaric medical procedures; the preservation of the integrity of the medical profession; the mitigation of fetal pain; and the prevention of discrimination on the basis of race, sex, or disability.

[These] legitimate interests justify Mississippi's Gestational Age Act. [The] Mississippi Legislature's findings recount the stages of "human prenatal development" and assert the State's interest in "protecting the life of the unborn." The legislature also found that abortions performed after 15 weeks typically use the dilation and evacuation procedure, and the legislature found the use of this procedure "for nontherapeutic or elective reasons [to be] a barbaric practice, dangerous for the maternal patient, and demeaning to the medical profession." These legitimate interests provide a rational basis for the Gestational Age Act, and it follows that respondents' constitutional challenge must fail.

[We] end this opinion where we began. Abortion presents a profound moral question. The Constitution does not prohibit the citizens of each State from regulating or prohibiting abortion. *Roe* and *Casey* arrogated that authority. We now overrule those decisions and return that authority to the people and their elected representatives.[1] * * *

JUSTICE THOMAS, concurring.

[I] write separately to emphasize [a] fundamental reason why there is no abortion guarantee lurking in the Due Process Clause. Considerable historical evidence indicates that "due process of law" merely required executive and judicial actors to comply with legislative enactments and the common law when depriving a person of life, liberty, or property. [In] future cases, we should reconsider all of this Court's substantive due process precedents, including *Griswold*, *Lawrence*, and *Obergefell*. [After] overruling these demonstrably erroneous decisions, the question would remain whether other constitutional provisions guarantee the myriad rights that our substantive due process cases have generated. [To] answer that question, we would need to decide important antecedent questions, including whether the Privileges or Immunities Clause protects *any* rights that are not enumerated in the Constitution and, if so, how to identify those rights. That said, even if the Clause does protect unenumerated rights, the Court conclusively demonstrates that abortion is not one of them under any plausible interpretive approach. * * *

JUSTICE KAVANAUGH, concurring.

[The] interests on both sides of the abortion issue are extraordinarily weighty. On the one side, many pro-choice advocates forcefully argue that the ability to obtain an abortion is critically important for women's personal and professional lives, and for women's health. They contend that

---

[1] Two appendices were attached to the majority opinion. Appendix A set forth "statutes criminalizing abortion at all stages of pregnancy in the States existing in 1968." Appendix B listed "statutes criminalizing abortion at all stages in each of the Territories that became States and in the District of Columbia."

the widespread availability of abortion has been essential for women to advance in society and to achieve greater equality over the last 50 years. And they maintain that women must have the freedom to choose for themselves whether to have an abortion. On the other side, many pro-life advocates forcefully argue that a fetus is a human life. They contend that all human life should be protected as a matter of human dignity and fundamental morality. And they stress that a significant percentage of Americans with pro-life views are women.

[The] Constitution does not take sides on the issue of abortion. The text of the Constitution does not refer to or encompass abortion. To be sure, this Court has held that the Constitution protects unenumerated rights that are deeply rooted in this Nation's history and tradition, and implicit in the concept of ordered liberty. But a right to abortion is not deeply rooted in American history and tradition, as the Court today thoroughly explains. [On] the question of abortion, the Constitution is therefore neither pro-life nor pro-choice. The Constitution is neutral and leaves the issue for the people and their elected representatives to resolve through the democratic process in the States or Congress. [Because] the Constitution is neutral on the issue of abortion, this Court also must be scrupulously neutral.

[Respondent] and its *amici* emphasize that the Constitution does not freeze the American people's rights as of 1791 or 1868. I fully agree. To begin, I agree that constitutional rights apply to situations that were unforeseen in 1791 or 1868—such as applying the First Amendment to the Internet or the Fourth Amendment to cars. Moreover, the Constitution authorizes the creation of new rights—state and federal, statutory and constitutional. But when it comes to creating new rights, the Constitution directs the people to the various processes of democratic self-government contemplated by the Constitution—state legislation, state constitutional amendments, federal legislation, and federal constitutional amendments. [This] Court therefore does not possess the authority either to declare a constitutional right to abortion *or* to declare a constitutional prohibition of abortion.

[The] fact that a precedent is wrong, even egregiously wrong, does not alone mean that the precedent should be overruled. But as the Court today explains, *Roe* has caused significant negative jurisprudential and real-world consequences. [The] *stare decisis* analysis here is somewhat more complicated because of *Casey*. But as has become increasingly evident over time, *Casey*'s well-intentioned effort did not resolve the abortion debate. The national division has not ended. In recent years, a significant number of States have enacted abortion restrictions that directly conflict with *Roe*. Those laws cannot be dismissed as political stunts or as outlier laws. Those numerous state laws collectively represent the sincere and deeply held views of tens of millions of Americans who continue to fervently believe that allowing abortions up to 24 weeks is far too radical and far too extreme, and does not sufficiently account for what *Roe* itself recognized as the State's "important and legitimate interest" in protecting fetal life. In this case, moreover, a majority of the States—26 in all—ask the Court to overrule *Roe* and return the abortion issue to the States. In short, *Casey's stare decisis* analysis rested in part on a predictive judgment about the future development of state laws and of the people's views on the abortion issue. But that predictive judgment has not borne out.

[After] today's decision, the nine Members of this Court will no longer decide the basic legality of pre-viability abortion for all 330 million Americans. That issue will be resolved by the people and their representatives in the democratic process in the States or Congress. But the parties' arguments have raised other related questions, and I address some of them here.

First is the question of how this decision will affect other precedents involving issues such as contraception and marriage—in particular, the decisions in *Griswold, Eisenstadt, Loving,* and *Obergefell*. I emphasize what the Court today states: Overruling *Roe* does *not* mean the overruling of those precedents, and does *not* threaten or cast doubt on those precedents.

Second, as I see it, some of the other abortion-related legal questions raised by today's decision are not especially difficult as a constitutional matter. For example, may a State bar a resident of that State from traveling to another State to obtain an abortion? In my view, the answer is no based on the constitutional right to interstate travel. May a State retroactively impose liability or punishment for an abortion that occurred before today's decision takes effect? In my view, the answer is no based on the Due Process Clause or the *Ex Post Facto* Clause. Cf. *Bouie v. City of Columbia*, 378 U.S. 347 (1964).

Other abortion-related legal questions may emerge in the future. But this Court will no longer decide the fundamental question of whether abortion must be allowed throughout the United States through 6 weeks, or 12 weeks, or 15 weeks, or 24 weeks, or some other line. The Court will no longer decide how to evaluate the interests of the pregnant woman and the interests in protecting fetal life throughout pregnancy. Instead, those difficult moral and policy questions will be decided, as the Constitution dictates, by the people and their elected representatives through the constitutional processes of democratic self-government. * * *

CHIEF JUSTICE ROBERTS, concurring in the judgment.

[I] agree with the Court that the viability line established by *Roe* and *Casey* should be discarded under a straightforward *stare decisis* analysis. That line never made any sense. Our abortion precedents describe the right at issue as a woman's right to choose to terminate her pregnancy. That right should therefore extend far enough to ensure a reasonable opportunity to choose, but need not extend any further—certainly not all the way to viability. Mississippi's law allows a woman three months to obtain an abortion, well beyond the point at which it is considered "late" to discover a pregnancy. [But] that is all I would say, out of adherence to a simple yet fundamental principle of judicial restraint: If it is not necessary to decide more to dispose of a case, then it is necessary *not* to decide more. Perhaps we are not always perfect in following that command, and certainly there are cases that warrant an exception. But this is not one of them. Surely we should adhere closely to principles of judicial restraint here, where the broader path the Court chooses entails repudiating a constitutional right we have not only previously recognized, but also expressly reaffirmed applying the doctrine of *stare decisis*. The Court's opinion is thoughtful and thorough, but those virtues cannot compensate for the fact that its dramatic and consequential ruling is unnecessary to decide the case before us.

[The] best defense of the viability line the *Casey* plurality could conjure up was workability. [Although] the plurality attempted to add more content by opining that "it might be said that a woman who fails to act before viability has consented to the State's intervention on behalf of the developing child," that mere suggestion provides no basis for choosing viability as the critical tipping point. A similar implied consent argument could be made with respect to a law banning abortions after fifteen weeks, well beyond the point at which nearly all women are aware that they are pregnant. The dissent, which would retain the viability line, offers no justification for it either.

[Consider] statutes passed in a number of jurisdictions that forbid abortions after twenty weeks of pregnancy, premised on the theory that a fetus can feel pain at that stage of development. Assuming that prevention of fetal pain is a legitimate state interest after *Gonzales v. Carhart*, 550 U.S. 124 (2007),[2] there seems to be no reason why viability would be relevant to the permissibility of such laws. The same is true of laws designed to "protect[ ] the integrity and ethics of the medical profession" and restrict procedures likely to "coarsen society" to the "dignity of human life." *Gonzales*. Mississippi's law, for instance, was premised in part on the legislature's finding that the "dilation and evacuation" procedure is a "barbaric practice, dangerous for the maternal patient, and demeaning to the medical profession." That procedure accounts for most abortions performed after the first trimester—two weeks before the period at issue in this case—and "involve[s] the use of surgical instruments to crush and tear the unborn child apart." Again, it would make little sense to focus on viability when evaluating a law based on these permissible goals. In short,

---

[2] In *Gonzales v. Carhart*, a 5–4 majority, per KENNEDY, J., upheld a federal law banning "partial birth abortion," defined as a method of abortion "that kills the partially delivered living fetus."

the viability rule was created outside the ordinary course of litigation, is and always has been completely unreasoned, and fails to take account of state interests since recognized as legitimate.

[None] of this, however, requires that we also take the dramatic step of altogether eliminating the abortion right first recognized in *Roe*. [Here], there is a clear path to deciding this case correctly without overruling *Roe* all the way down to the studs: recognize that the viability line must be discarded, as the majority rightly does, and leave for another day whether to reject any right to an abortion at all.

[Both] the Court's opinion and the dissent display a relentless freedom from doubt on the legal issue that I cannot share. I am not sure, for example, that a ban on terminating a pregnancy from the moment of conception must be treated the same under the Constitution as a ban after fifteen weeks. [I] would decide the question we granted review to answer— whether the previously recognized abortion right bars all abortion restrictions prior to viability, such that a ban on abortions after fifteen weeks of pregnancy is necessarily unlawful. The answer to that question is no, and there is no need to go further to decide this case. I therefore concur only in the judgment.

JUSTICE BREYER, JUSTICE SOTOMAYOR, and JUSTICE KAGAN, dissenting.

For half a century, *Roe* and *Casey* have protected the liberty and equality of women. *Roe* held, and *Casey* reaffirmed, that the Constitution safeguards a woman's right to decide for herself whether to bear a child. *Roe* held, and *Casey* reaffirmed, that in the first stages of pregnancy, the government could not make that choice for women. The government could not control a woman's body or the course of a woman's life: It could not determine what the woman's future would be. Respecting a woman as an autonomous being, and granting her full equality, meant giving her substantial choice over this most personal and most consequential of all life decisions.

Roe and *Casey* well understood the difficulty and divisiveness of the abortion issue. The Court knew that Americans hold profoundly different views about the "moral[ity]" of "terminating a pregnancy, even in its earliest stage." *Casey*. And the Court recognized that "the State has legitimate interests from the outset of the pregnancy in protecting" the "life of the fetus that may become a child." So the Court struck a balance, as it often does when values and goals compete. [Today], the Court discards that balance. It says that from the very moment of fertilization, a woman has no rights to speak of. A State can force her to bring a pregnancy to term, even at the steepest personal and familial costs. An abortion restriction, the majority holds, is permissible whenever rational, the lowest level of scrutiny known to the law. And because, as the Court has often stated, protecting fetal life is rational, States will feel free to enact all manner of restrictions.

The Mississippi law at issue here bars abortions after the 15th week of pregnancy. Under the majority's ruling, though, another State's law could do so after ten weeks, or five or three or one—or, again, from the moment of fertilization. States have already passed such laws, in anticipation of today's ruling. More will follow. Some States have enacted laws extending to all forms of abortion procedure, including taking medication in one's own home. They have passed laws without any exceptions for when the woman is the victim of rape or incest. Under those laws, a woman will have to bear her rapist's child or a young girl her father's—no matter if doing so will destroy her life. So too, after today's ruling, some States may compel women to carry to term a fetus with severe physical anomalies—for example, one afflicted with Tay-Sachs disease, sure to die within a few years of birth. States may even argue that a prohibition on abortion need make no provision for protecting a woman from risk of death or physical harm. Across a vast array of circumstances, a State will be able to impose its moral choice on a woman and coerce her to give birth to a child.

[The] majority tries to hide the geographically expansive effects of its holding. Today's decision, the majority says, permits "each State" to address abortion as it pleases. That is cold comfort, of course, for the poor woman who cannot get the money to fly to a distant State for a procedure. Above all others, women lacking financial resources will suffer from today's decision. In any event, interstate restrictions will also soon be in the offing. After this decision, some States may block women from traveling out of State to obtain abortions, or even from receiving abortion medications from out of State. Some may criminalize efforts, including the provision of information or funding, to help women gain access to other States' abortion services. Most threatening of all, no language in today's decision stops the Federal Government from prohibiting abortions nationwide, once again from the moment of conception and without exceptions for rape or incest.

[As] of today, this Court holds, a State can always force a woman to give birth, prohibiting even the earliest abortions. A State can thus transform what, when freely undertaken, is a wonder into what, when forced, may be a nightmare. Some women, especially women of means, will find ways around the State's assertion of power. Others—those without money or childcare or the ability to take time off from work—will not be so fortunate. Maybe they will try an unsafe method of abortion, and come to physical harm, or even die. Maybe they will undergo pregnancy and have a child, but at significant personal or familial cost. At the least, they will incur the cost of losing control of their lives. The Constitution will, today's majority holds, provide no shield, despite its guarantees of liberty and equality for all.

And no one should be confident that this majority is done with its work. The right *Roe* and *Casey* recognized does not stand alone. To the contrary, the Court has linked it for decades to other settled freedoms involving bodily integrity, familial relationships, and procreation. Most obviously, the right to terminate a pregnancy arose straight out of the right to purchase and use contraception. See *Griswold*; *Eisenstadt*. In turn, those rights led, more recently, to rights of same-sex intimacy and marriage. See *Lawrence*; *Obergefell*. They are all part of the same constitutional fabric, protecting autonomous decisionmaking over the most personal of life decisions. The majority [tells] us today that nothing it does "cast[s] doubt on precedents that do not concern abortion." But how could that be? The lone rationale for what the majority does today is that the right to elect an abortion is not "deeply rooted in history": Not until *Roe*, the majority argues, did people think abortion fell within the Constitution's guarantee of liberty. The same could be said, though, of most of the rights the majority claims it is not tampering with. The majority could write just as long an opinion showing, for example, that until the mid-20th century, "there was no support in American law for a constitutional right to obtain [contraceptives]." So one of two things must be true. Either the majority does not really believe in its own reasoning. Or if it does, all rights that have no history stretching back to the mid-19th century are insecure. Either the mass of the majority's opinion is hypocrisy, or additional constitutional rights are under threat.

[To] hear the majority tell the tale, *Roe* and *Casey* are aberrations: They came from nowhere, went nowhere—and so are easy to excise from this Nation's constitutional law. That is not true. [They] are rooted in—and themselves led to—other rights giving individuals control over their bodies and their most personal and intimate associations. The majority does not wish to talk about these matters for obvious reasons; to do so would both ground *Roe* and *Casey* in this Court's precedents and reveal the broad implications of today's decision.

[The] majority's insistence that *Roe* and *Casey* [dismiss] a "State's interest in protecting prenatal life" [gets] those decisions [badly] wrong. [*Roe*] and *Casey* invoked powerful state interests in that protection, operative at every stage of the pregnancy and overriding the woman's liberty after viability. The strength of those state interests is exactly why the Court allowed greater restrictions on the abortion right than on other rights deriving from the Fourteenth Amendment. But what *Roe* and *Casey* also recognized—which today's majority does not—is that a woman's freedom and equality are likewise involved. That fact—the presence of countervailing interests—is what made the abortion question hard, and what necessitated balancing. [The] majority would allow States to ban abortion from conception onward because it does not think forced childbirth at all implicates a woman's rights to equality and freedom. Today's Court, that is, does not think there is anything of constitutional significance attached to a woman's control of her body and the path of her life. *Roe* and *Casey* thought that one-sided view misguided. In some sense, that is the difference in a nutshell between our precedents and the majority opinion. The constitutional regime we have lived in for the last 50 years recognized competing interests, and sought a balance between them. The constitutional regime we enter today erases the woman's interest and recognizes only the State's (or the Federal Government's).

[The] majority makes this change based on a single question: Did the reproductive right recognized in *Roe* and *Casey* exist in "1868, the year when the Fourteenth Amendment was ratified"? The majority says (and with this much we agree) that the answer to this question is no: In 1868, there was no nationwide right to end a pregnancy, and no thought that the Fourteenth Amendment provided one.

The majority's core legal postulate, then, is that we in the 21st century must read the Fourteenth Amendment just as its ratifiers did. [If] the ratifiers did not understand something as central to freedom, then neither can we. Or said more particularly: If those people did not understand reproductive rights as part of the guarantee of liberty conferred in the Fourteenth Amendment, then those rights do not exist.

[Note] a mistake in the just preceding sentence. We referred there to the "people" who ratified the Fourteenth Amendment: What rights did those "people" have in their heads at the time? But, of course, "people" did not ratify the Fourteenth Amendment. Men did. So it is perhaps not so surprising that the ratifiers were not perfectly attuned to the importance of reproductive rights for women's liberty, or for their capacity to participate as equal members of our Nation. [Those] responsible for the original Constitution, including the Fourteenth Amendment, did not perceive women as equals, and did not recognize women's rights. When the majority says that we must read our foundational charter as viewed at the time of ratification (except that we may also check it against the Dark Ages), it consigns women to second-class citizenship.

So how is it that, as *Casey* said, our Constitution, read now, grants rights to women, though it did not in 1868? How is it that our Constitution subjects discrimination against them to heightened judicial scrutiny? How is it that our Constitution, through the Fourteenth Amendment's liberty clause, guarantees access to contraception (also not legally protected in 1868) so that women can decide for themselves whether and when to bear a child? How is it that until today, that same constitutional clause protected a woman's right, in the event contraception failed, to end a pregnancy in its earlier stages? The answer is that this Court has rejected the majority's pinched view of how to read our Constitution. [Our] Constitution is "intended to endure for ages to come," and must adapt itself to a future "seen dimly," if at all. *McCulloch v. Maryland* [Ch. 2, Sec. 1, supra]. That is indeed why our Constitution is written as it is. The Framers (both in 1788 and 1868) understood that the world changes. So they did not define rights by reference to the specific practices existing at the time. Instead, the Framers defined rights in general terms, to permit future evolution in their scope and meaning. And over the course of our history, this Court has taken up the Framers' invitation. It has kept true to the Framers' principles by applying them in new ways, responsive to new societal understandings and conditions.

Nowhere has that approach been more prevalent than in construing the majestic but open-ended words of the Fourteenth Amendment—the guarantees of "liberty" and "equality" for all. And nowhere has that approach produced prouder moments, for this country and the Court. [The] Fourteenth Amendment's ratifiers did not think it gave black and white people a right to marry each other. To the contrary, contemporaneous practice deemed that act quite as unprotected as abortion. Yet the Court in *Loving* read the Fourteenth Amendment to embrace the Lovings' union.

[That] does not mean anything goes. The majority wishes people to think there are but two alternatives: (1) accept the original applications of the Fourteenth Amendment and no others, or (2) surrender to judges' "own ardent views," ungrounded in law, about the "liberty that Americans should enjoy." [But] applications of liberty and equality can evolve while remaining grounded in constitutional principles, constitutional history, and constitutional precedents. The second Justice Harlan discussed how to strike the right balance when he explained why he would have invalidated a State's ban on contraceptive use. Judges, he said, are not "free to roam where unguided speculation might take them." *Poe* (dissenting opinion).

It was settled at the time of *Roe*, settled at the time of *Casey*, and settled yesterday that the Constitution places limits on a State's power to assert control over an individual's body and most personal decisionmaking. A multitude of decisions supporting that principle led to *Roe*'s recognition and *Casey*'s reaffirmation of the right to choose; and *Roe* and *Casey* in turn supported additional protections for intimate and familial relations. [And] eliminating that right [is] not taking a "neutral" position, as Justice Kavanaugh tries to argue. [Would] he say that the Court is being "scrupulously neutral" if it allowed New York and California to ban all the guns they want? If the Court allowed some States to use unanimous juries and others not? If the Court told the States: Decide for yourselves whether to put restrictions on church attendance?

[There] are few greater incursions on a body than forcing a woman to complete a pregnancy and give birth. For every woman, those experiences involve all manner of physical changes, medical treatments (including the possibility of a cesarean section), and medical risk. Just as one example, an

American woman is 14 times more likely to die by carrying a pregnancy to term than by having an abortion. That women happily undergo those burdens and hazards of their own accord does not lessen how far a State impinges on a woman's body when it compels her to bring a pregnancy to term. And for some women, as *Roe* recognized, abortions are medically necessary to prevent harm. The majority does not say—which is itself ominous—whether a State may prevent a woman from obtaining an abortion when she and her doctor have determined it is a needed medical treatment.

[*Casey* also] made clear that the precedents *Roe* most closely tracked were those involving contraception. Over the course of three cases, the Court had held that a right to use and gain access to contraception was part of the Fourteenth Amendment's guarantee of liberty. That clause, we explained, necessarily conferred a right "to be free from unwarranted governmental intrusion into matters so fundamentally affecting a person as the decision whether to bear or beget a child." *Eisenstadt.*

[Faced] with all these connections between *Roe/Casey* and judicial decisions recognizing other constitutional rights, the majority tells everyone not to worry. It can (so it says) neatly extract the right to choose from the constitutional edifice without affecting any associated rights. (Think of someone telling you that the Jenga tower simply will not collapse.) Should the audience for these too-much-repeated protestations be duly satisfied? We think not.

The first problem with the majority's account comes from Justice Thomas's concurrence—which makes clear he is not with the program. "[I]n future cases," he says, "we should reconsider all of this Court's substantive due process precedents, including *Griswold, Lawrence,* and *Obergefell.*" [Then] "we have a duty" to "overrul[e] these demonstrably erroneous decisions." So at least one Justice is planning to use the ticket of today's decision again and again and again.

[Nor] does it even help just to take the majority at its word. Assume the majority is sincere in saying, for whatever reason, that it will go so far and no further. Scout's honor. Still, the future significance of today's opinion will be decided in the future.

[Today's] decision, taken on its own, is catastrophic enough. [The] majority's opinion has all the flaws its method would suggest. Because laws in 1868 deprived women of any control over their bodies, the majority approves States doing so today. Because those laws prevented women from charting the course of their own lives, the majority says States can do the same again. Because in 1868, the government could tell a pregnant woman—even in the first days of her pregnancy—that she could do nothing but bear a child, it can once more impose that command. Today's decision strips women of agency over what even the majority agrees is a contested and contestable moral issue. It forces her to carry out the State's will, whatever the circumstances and whatever the harm it will wreak on her and her family. In the Fourteenth Amendment's terms, it takes away her liberty.

[The] majority has overruled *Roe* and *Casey* for one and only one reason: because it has always despised them, and now it has the votes to discard them. The majority thereby substitutes a rule by judges for the rule of law.

[Contrary] to the majority's view, there is nothing unworkable about *Casey*'s "undue burden" standard. General standards, like the undue burden standard, are ubiquitous in the law, and particularly in constitutional adjudication. When called on to give effect to the Constitution's broad principles, this Court often crafts flexible standards that can be applied case-by-case to a myriad of unforeseeable circumstances. Applying general standards to particular cases is, in many contexts, just what it means to do law.

[Anyone] concerned about workability should consider the majority's substitute standard. [This] Court will surely face critical questions about how [the rational basis] test applies. Must a state law allow abortions when necessary to protect a woman's life and health? And if so, exactly when? How much risk to a woman's life can a State force her to incur, before the Fourteenth Amendment's protection of life kicks in? Suppose a patient with pulmonary hypertension has a 30-to-50 percent risk of dying with ongoing pregnancy; is that enough? And short of death, how much illness or injury can the State require her to accept, consistent with the Amendment's protection of liberty and equality? Further, the Court may face questions about the application of abortion regulations to medical care most people view as quite different from abortion. What about the morning-after pill? IUDs? In vitro fertilization? And how about the use of dilation and evacuation or medication for miscarriage management?

[The] majority's ruling today invites a host of questions about interstate conflicts. Can a State bar women from traveling to another State to obtain an abortion? Can a State prohibit advertising out-of-state abortions or helping women get to out-of-state providers? Can a State interfere with the mailing of drugs used for medication abortions? The Constitution protects travel and speech and interstate commerce, so today's ruling will give rise to a host of new constitutional questions.

[*Roe*] and *Casey* continue to reflect, not diverge from, broad trends in American society. It is, of course, true that many Americans, including many women, opposed those decisions when issued and do so now as well. Yet the fact remains: *Roe* and *Casey* were the product of a profound and ongoing change in women's roles in the latter part of the 20th century. Only a dozen years before *Roe*, the Court described women as "the center of home and family life," with "special responsibilities" that precluded their full legal status under the Constitution. *Hoyt v. Florida* [Ch. 9, Sec. 3, I, infra]. By 1973, when the Court decided *Roe*, fundamental social change was underway regarding the place of women—and the law had begun to follow. [By] 1992, when the Court decided *Casey*, the traditional view of a woman's role as only a wife and mother was "no longer consistent with our understanding of the family, the individual, or the Constitution." Under that charter, *Casey* understood, women must take their place as full and equal citizens. And for that to happen, women must have control over their reproductive decisions. Nothing since *Casey*—no changed law, no changed fact—has undermined that promise.

[About] 18 percent of pregnancies in this country end in abortion, and about one quarter of American women will have an abortion before the age of 45. Those numbers reflect the predictable and life-changing effects of carrying a pregnancy, giving birth, and becoming a parent. As *Casey* understood, people today rely on their ability to control and time pregnancies when making countless life decisions: where to live, whether and how to invest in education or careers, how to allocate financial resources, and how to approach intimate and family relationships. Women may count on abortion access for when contraception fails. They may count on abortion access for when contraception cannot be used, for example, if they were raped. They may count on abortion for when something changes in the midst of a pregnancy, whether it involves family or financial circumstances, unanticipated medical complications, or heartbreaking fetal diagnoses. Taking away the right to abortion, as the majority does today, destroys all those individual plans and expectations. In so doing, it diminishes women's opportunities to participate fully and equally in the Nation's political, social, and economic life. See Brief for Economists as *Amici Curiae* (showing that abortion availability has "large effects on women's education, labor force participation, occupations, and earnings").

[The] Court's failure to perceive the whole swath of expectations *Roe* and *Casey* created reflects an impoverished view of reliance. [By] disclaiming any need to consider broad swaths of individuals' interests, the Court arrogates to itself the authority to overrule established legal principles without even acknowledging the costs of its decisions for the individuals who live under the law, costs that this Court's *stare decisis* doctrine instructs us to privilege when deciding whether to change course. [After] today, young women will come of age with fewer rights than their mothers and grandmothers had. The majority accomplishes that result without so much as considering how women have relied on the right to choose or what it means to take that right away. The majority's refusal even to consider the life-altering consequences of reversing *Roe* and *Casey* is a stunning indictment of its decision.

[With] sorrow—for this Court, but more, for the many millions of American women who have today lost a fundamental constitutional protection—we dissent.[3]

NOTES AND QUESTIONS

1.   *Distinguishing other rights.* The *Dobbs* dissent and arguably the concurrence of Justice Thomas say that the rationale of the majority opinion has far-reaching implications beyond abortion rights, including for contraception and same-sex marriage. The majority and Justice Kavanaugh's concurrence contest this inference, noting that none of the other substantive due process rights involves the deliberate killing of a "potential life" or "unborn human being." How effective is this rejoinder, given the majority's chiefly historical methodology? Would it be more persuasive if the Court had overruled *Roe* and *Casey* on the ground that the government's compelling interest justifies overriding the fundamental rights at issue in abortion, rather than holding, as the majority did, that there is no fundamental right in the first place?

2.   *Judicial politics.* The Court states that "*Roe* and *Casey* have enflamed debate and deepened division." Finley (note 10 after *Roe*, supra) contests that claim, and whether abortion politics would have been calmer had the Court never found a constitutional right to abortion is ultimately unknowable. But surely the cases impacted politics concerning the Supreme Court itself. Just under two months before the official release of *Dobbs*, the online magazine *Politico* published a leaked draft of the majority opinion, which the Court quickly confirmed as authentic. The leak sparked an internal investigation into the source, further leaks about an atmosphere of mistrust at the Court, public protests at the homes of Justices in the majority, and the arrest of a man who appeared to be planning to assassinate Justice Kavanaugh. After the opinion's formal release, Democratic Senator Joe Manchin of West Virginia and Republican Senator Susan Collins of Maine both complained that Justices Gorsuch and Kavanaugh—whom they had each voted to confirm—had testified dishonestly during their respective confirmation hearings by describing *Roe* and *Casey* as settled law that they had no intention of overruling. The impact of *Dobbs* on future confirmation hearings remains to be seen.

3.   *Federalism.* Following *Dobbs*, abortion law varies greatly from state to state, but as the dissent observes, in ceding authority over abortion regulation to "the people and their elected representatives," the majority leaves open the possibility of legislation by Congress. Would a federal law either restoring abortion rights as a matter of statute or banning abortions nationwide be constitutional? Note that lower courts have uniformly upheld

---

[3]   In response to footnote 48 of the majority opinion, the dissent included an appendix analyzing "in full each of the 28 cases the majority" cited in support of its "decision to overrule" *Roe* and *Casey*, adding that "the Court in each case relied on traditional *stare decisis* factors in overruling."

the Freedom of Access to Clinic Entrances Act, 18 U.S.C. § 248, which provides criminal and civil penalties for blocking access to or otherwise interfering with a facility that "provides reproductive health services." See United States v. Weslin, 156 F.3d 292, 295 (2dCir.1998)(collecting appeals court cases); see also note 2(d) after *Gonzales v. Raich* (Ch. 2, Sec. 2, IV, supra). Consider, however, that when, in *Gonzales v. Carhart,* supra, the Court sustained the federal Partial-Birth Abortion Ban Act, 18 U.S.C. § 1531, against a challenge based on *Roe* and *Casey,* Thomas, J., joined by Scalia, J., concurred but added that the question whether the Act "constitutes a permissible exercise of Congress' power under the Commerce Clause is not before the Court." In the event that a future Congress were to ban abortion nationwide, how likely is it that a hybrid challenge to the law would result in its invalidation by appealing to a coalition among, on one hand, Justices who would reverse *Dobbs* and reinstate *Roe/Casey* and, on the other hand, Justices (like Justice Thomas) who generally take a narrow view of Congressional power under the Commerce Clause?

4. SEXUAL LIBERTY

P. 527, replace the second paragraph of note 9 with:

10. ***Is Lawrence consistent with Dobbs?*** In *Dobbs,* supra, the Court relied extensively on the *Glucksberg* test. Does that reliance imperil the right recognized in *Lawrence* and other substantive due process rights that are not deeply rooted in American history and tradition at the level of specificity *Glucksberg* seemingly requires? So said the *Dobbs* dissenters. The majority opinion of Alito, J., in *Dobbs* called such fears "unfounded," noting that unlike abortion, the exercise of the right protected by *Lawrence* and other cases "does not destroy a 'potential life.' " It is unclear, however, why that fact bears on whether to recognize a right, rather than whether the state has a compelling interest in overriding the right. Meanwhile, Thomas, J., concurring in *Dobbs,* expressly urged the overruling of *Lawrence* and other substantive due process cases.

7. THE RIGHT TO KEEP AND BEAR ARMS

Pp. 586–87, delete notes 5 and 6 as well as the note on *Caetano v. Massachusetts,* then add immediately before Section 8:

NEW YORK STATE RIFLE & PISTOL ASS'N, INC. V. BRUEN
___ U.S. ___, 142 S.Ct. 2111, ___ L.Ed.2d ___ (2022).

JUSTICE THOMAS delivered the opinion of the Court.

In *Heller* and *McDonald,* we recognized that the Second and Fourteenth Amendments protect the right of an ordinary, law-abiding citizen to possess a handgun in the home for self-defense. In this case, petitioners and respondents agree that ordinary, law-abiding citizens have a similar right to carry handguns publicly for their self-defense. We too agree, and now hold, consistent with *Heller* and *McDonald*, that the Second and Fourteenth Amendments protect an individual's right to carry a handgun for self-defense outside the home.

[In] 43 States, the government issues licenses to carry based on objective criteria. But in six States, including New York, the government further conditions issuance of a license to carry on a citizen's showing of some additional special need. [We] conclude that the State's licensing regime violates the Constitution.

[New York's current] licensing scheme largely tracks that of the early 1900s. It is a crime in New York to possess "any firearm" without a license, whether inside or outside the home, punishable by up to four years in prison or a $5,000 fine for a felony offense, and one year in prison or a $1,000 fine for a misdemeanor. Meanwhile, possessing a loaded firearm outside one's home or place of business without a license is a felony punishable by up to 15 years in prison. A license applicant who wants to possess a firearm [outside] his home or place of business for self-defense [must] obtain an unrestricted license to "have and carry" a concealed "pistol or revolver." To secure that license, the applicant must prove that "proper cause exists" to issue it. [No] New York statute defines "proper cause." But New York courts have held that an applicant shows proper cause only if he can "demonstrate a special need for self-protection distinguishable from that of the general community." [New] York courts generally require evidence "of particular threats, attacks or other extraordinary danger to personal safety." [New] York courts defer to an officer's application of the proper-cause standard unless it is "arbitrary and capricious."

[New] York is not alone in requiring a permit to carry a handgun in public. But the vast majority of States [are] "shall issue" jurisdictions, where authorities must issue concealed-carry licenses whenever applicants satisfy certain threshold requirements, without granting licensing officials discretion to deny licenses based on a perceived lack of need or suitability.

[In] the years since [*Heller* and *McDonald*], the Courts of Appeals have coalesced around a "two-step" framework for analyzing Second Amendment challenges that combines history with means-end scrutiny. [The] Courts of Appeals [first] ascertain the original scope of the right based on its historical meaning. If [the] historical evidence at this step is "inconclusive or suggests that the regulated activity is *not* categorically unprotected," the courts generally proceed to step two. [If] a "core" Second Amendment right is burdened, courts apply "strict scrutiny" and ask whether the Government can prove that the law is "narrowly tailored to achieve a compelling governmental interest." Otherwise, they apply intermediate scrutiny and consider whether the Government can show that the regulation is "substantially related to the achievement of an important governmental interest."

[Despite] the popularity of this two-step approach, it is one step too many. Step one of the predominant framework is broadly consistent with *Heller*, which demands a test rooted in the Second Amendment's text, as informed by history. But *Heller* and *McDonald* do not support applying means-end scrutiny in the Second Amendment context. Instead, the government must affirmatively prove that its firearms regulation is part of the historical tradition that delimits the outer bounds of the right to keep and bear arms.

[This] Second Amendment standard accords with how we protect other constitutional rights. Take, for instance, the freedom of speech in the First Amendment, to which *Heller* repeatedly compared the right to keep and bear arms. In that context, "[w]hen the Government restricts speech, the Government bears the burden of proving the constitutionality of its actions." In some cases, that burden includes showing whether the expressive conduct falls outside of the category of protected speech. And to carry that burden, the government must generally point to *historical* evidence about the reach of the First Amendment's protections. See, *e.g.*, *United States v. Stevens* [Ch. 7, Sec. 4, III, infra] (placing the burden on the government to show that a type of speech belongs to a "historic and traditional categor[y]" of constitutionally unprotected speech "long familiar to the bar."

And beyond the freedom of speech, our focus on history also comports with how we assess many other constitutional claims. If a litigant asserts the [Sixth Amendment] right in court to "be confronted with the witnesses against him," we require courts to consult history to determine the scope of that right. [Similarly], when a litigant claims a violation of his rights under the Establishment Clause, [we] look to history for guidance. We adopt a similar approach here.

[If] the last decade of Second Amendment litigation has taught this Court anything, it is that federal courts tasked with making such difficult empirical judgments regarding firearm regulations under the banner of "intermediate scrutiny" often defer to the determinations of legislatures. But while that judicial deference to legislative interest balancing is understandable—and, elsewhere, appropriate—it is not deference that the Constitution demands here.

[When] a challenged regulation addresses a general societal problem that has persisted since the 18th century, the lack of a distinctly similar historical regulation addressing that problem is relevant evidence that the challenged regulation is inconsistent with the Second Amendment. Likewise, if earlier generations addressed the societal problem, but did so through materially different means, that also could be evidence that a modern regulation is unconstitutional. And if some jurisdictions actually attempted to enact analogous regulations during this timeframe, but those proposals were rejected on constitutional grounds, that rejection surely would provide some probative evidence of unconstitutionality.

[Much] like we use history to determine which modern "arms" are protected by the Second Amendment, so too does history guide our consideration of modern regulations that were unimaginable at the founding. When confronting such present-day firearm regulations, this historical inquiry that courts must conduct will often involve reasoning by analogy—a commonplace task for any lawyer or judge. [While] we do not now provide an exhaustive survey of the features that render regulations relevantly similar under the Second Amendment, we do think that *Heller* and *McDonald* point toward at least two metrics: how and why the regulations burden a law-abiding citizen's right to armed self-defense.

[We] think respondents err in their attempt to characterize New York's proper-cause requirement as a "sensitive-place" law. In their view, "sensitive places" where the government may lawfully disarm law-abiding citizens include all "places where people typically congregate and where law-enforcement and other public-safety professionals are presumptively available." It is true that people sometimes congregate in "sensitive places," and it is likewise true that law enforcement professionals are usually presumptively available in those locations. But expanding the category of "sensitive places" simply to all places of public congregation that are not isolated from law enforcement defines the category of "sensitive places" far too broadly. Respondents' argument would in effect exempt cities from the Second Amendment and would eviscerate the general right to publicly carry arms for self-defense that we discuss in detail below. Put simply, there is no historical basis for New York to effectively declare the island of Manhattan a "sensitive place" simply because it is crowded and protected generally by the New York City Police Department.

[To] confine the right to "bear" arms to the home would nullify half of the Second Amendment's operative protections. Moreover, confining the right to "bear" arms to the home would make little sense given that self-defense is "the *central component* of the [Second Amendment] right itself." Although we remarked in *Heller* that the need for armed self-defense is perhaps "most acute" in the home, we did not suggest that the need was insignificant elsewhere. Many Americans hazard greater danger outside the home than in it. [The] text of the Second Amendment reflects that reality. The Second Amendment's plain text thus presumptively guarantees petitioners [a] right to "bear" arms in public for self-defense.

[Respondents] appeal to a variety of historical sources from the late 1200s to the early 1900s. We categorize these periods as follows: (1) medieval to early modern England; (2) the American Colonies and the early

Republic; (3) antebellum America; (4) Reconstruction; and (5) the late-19th and early-20th centuries.

[When] it comes to interpreting the Constitution, not all history is created equal. "Constitutional rights are enshrined with the scope they were understood to have *when the people adopted them*." *Heller* (emphasis added). The Second Amendment was adopted in 1791; the Fourteenth in 1868. Historical evidence that long predates either date may not illuminate the scope of the right if linguistic or legal conventions changed in the intervening years.

[Throughout] modern Anglo-American history, the right to keep and bear arms in public has traditionally been subject to well-defined restrictions governing the intent for which one could carry arms, the manner of carry, or the exceptional circumstances under which one could not carry arms. But apart from a handful of late-19th-century jurisdictions, the historical record compiled by respondents does not demonstrate a tradition of broadly prohibiting the public carry of commonly used firearms for self-defense. Nor is there any such historical tradition limiting public carry only to those law-abiding citizens who demonstrate a special need for self-defense.[9] We conclude that respondents have failed to meet their burden to identify an American tradition justifying New York's proper-cause requirement. Under *Heller*'s text-and-history standard, the proper-cause requirement is therefore unconstitutional.

1

[We find] the English history that respondents and the United States muster [ambiguous] at best and see little reason to think that the Framers would have thought it applicable in the New World. It is not sufficiently probative to defend New York's proper-cause requirement.

[Respondents] argue that the prohibition on "rid[ing]" or "go[ing] . . . armed" [in the 1328 Statute of Northampton] was a sweeping restriction on public carry of self-defense weapons that would ultimately be adopted in Colonial America and justify onerous public-carry regulations. [However,] the Statute of Northampton—at least as it was understood

---

[9] **[Ct's Note]** [Nothing] in our analysis should be interpreted to suggest the unconstitutionality of the 43 States' "shall-issue" licensing regimes). [Because] these licensing regimes do not require applicants to show an atypical need for armed self-defense, they do not necessarily prevent "law-abiding, responsible citizens" from exercising their Second Amendment right to public carry. *Heller*. Rather, it appears that these shall-issue regimes, which often require applicants to undergo a background check or pass a firearms safety course, are designed to ensure only that those bearing arms in the jurisdiction are, in fact, "law-abiding, responsible citizens." And they likewise appear to contain only "narrow, objective, and definite standards" guiding licensing officials, *Shuttlesworth v. Birmingham*, 394 U.S. 147 (1969), rather than requiring the "appraisal of facts, the exercise of judgment, and the formation of an opinion," *Cantwell v. Connecticut* [Ch. 7, Sec. 2, I, infra]—features that typify proper-cause standards like New York's. That said, because any permitting scheme can be put toward abusive ends, we do not rule out constitutional challenges to shall-issue regimes where, for example, lengthy wait times in processing license applications or exorbitant fees deny ordinary citizens their right to public carry.

during the Middle Ages—has little bearing on the Second Amendment adopted in 1791. The Statute of Northampton was enacted nearly 20 years before the Black Death, more than 200 years before the birth of Shakespeare, more than 350 years before the Salem Witch Trials, more than 450 years before the ratification of the Constitution, and nearly 550 years before the adoption of the Fourteenth Amendment.

The Statute's prohibition on going or riding "armed" obviously did not contemplate handguns, given they did not appear in Europe until about the mid-1500s. [The] Statute's apparent focus on armor and, perhaps, weapons like [lances] given that armor and lances were generally worn or carried only when one intended to engage in lawful combat or—as most early violations of the Statute show—to breach the peace. [Respondents] point to no evidence suggesting the Statute applied to the smaller medieval weapons that strike us as most analogous to modern handguns. [Henry] VIII issued several proclamations decrying the proliferation of handguns, and Parliament passed several statutes restricting their possession. [But] Henry VIII's displeasure with handguns arose not primarily from concerns about their safety but rather their inefficacy. Henry VIII [and later James I] worried that handguns threatened Englishmen's proficiency with the longbow. [And] by the time Englishmen began to arrive in America in the early 1600s, the public carry of handguns was no longer widely proscribed.

When we look to the latter half of the 17th century, respondents' case only weakens. [Parliament wrote] the "predecessor to our Second Amendment" into the 1689 English Bill of Rights, *Heller*, guaranteeing that "Protestants . . . may have Arms for their Defence suitable to their Conditions, and as allowed by Law," 1 Wm. & Mary c. 2, § 7, in 3 Eng. Stat. at Large 417 (1689). Although this right was initially limited—it was restricted to Protestants and held only against the Crown, but not Parliament—it represented a watershed in English history. [Thus], whatever place handguns had in English society during the Tudor and Stuart reigns, by the time we reach the 18th century—and near the founding—they had gained a fairly secure footing in English culture. At the very least, we cannot conclude from this historical record that, by the time of the founding, English law would have justified restricting the right to publicly bear arms suited for self-defense only to those who demonstrate some special need for self-protection.

2

Respondents next point us to the history of the Colonies and early Republic, but there is little evidence of an early American practice of regulating public carry by the general public. This should come as no surprise—English subjects founded the Colonies at about the time England had itself begun to eliminate restrictions on the ownership and use of handguns. In the colonial era, respondents point to only three restrictions on public carry. For starters, we doubt that *three* colonial regulations could suffice to show a tradition of public-carry regulation. In any event, even looking at these laws on their own terms, we are not convinced that they regulated public carry akin to the New York law before us.

Two of the statutes were substantively identical. Colonial Massachusetts and New Hampshire both authorized justices of the peace to arrest "all Affrayers, Rioters, Disturbers, or Breakers of the Peace, and such as shall ride or go armed Offensively . . . by Night or by Day, in Fear or Affray of Their Majesties Liege People." 1692 Mass. Acts and Laws no. 6, pp. 11–12; see 1699 N. H. Acts and Laws ch. 1. [Respondents], their *amici*, and the dissent all misunderstand these statutes. Far from banning the carrying of any class of firearms, they merely codified the existing common-law offense of bearing arms to terrorize the people, as had the Statute of Northampton itself.

[Even] if respondents' reading of these colonial statutes were correct, it would still do little to support restrictions on the public carry of handguns *today*. At most, respondents can show that colonial legislatures sometimes prohibited the carrying of "dangerous and unusual weapons"—a fact we already acknowledged in *Heller*. [Thus], even if these colonial laws prohibited the carrying of handguns because they were considered "dangerous and unusual weapons" in the 1690s, they provide no justification for laws restricting the public carry of weapons that are unquestionably in common use today.

The third statute invoked by respondents was enacted in East New Jersey in 1686. It prohibited the concealed carry of "pocket pistol[s]" or other "unusual or unlawful weapons," and it further prohibited "planter[s]" from carrying all pistols unless in military service or, if "strangers," when traveling through the Province. An Act Against Wearing Swords, &c., ch. 9, in *Grants, Concessions, and Original Constitutions of the Province of New Jersey* 290 (2d ed. 1881) (Grants and Concessions). These restrictions do not meaningfully support respondents. The law restricted only concealed carry, not all public carry, and its restrictions applied only to certain "unusual or unlawful weapons," including "pocket pistol[s]." It also did not apply to all pistols, let alone all firearms. "Pocket pistols" had barrel lengths of perhaps 3 or 4 inches, far smaller than the 6-inch to 14-inch barrels found on the other belt and hip pistols that were commonly used for lawful purposes in the 1600s. [In] any event, we cannot put meaningful weight on this solitary statute.

Respondents next direct our attention to three late-18th-century and early-19th-century statutes, but each parallels the colonial statutes already discussed. [They] prohibit bearing arms in a way that spreads "fear" or "terror" among the people. [All] told, in the century leading up to the Second Amendment and in the first decade after its adoption, there is no historical basis for concluding that the pre-existing right enshrined in the Second Amendment permitted broad prohibitions on all forms of public carry.

3

Only after the ratification of the Second Amendment in 1791 did public-carry restrictions proliferate. [There] is no evidence indicating that the common-law limitations impaired the right of the general population to peaceable public carry. For example, the Tennessee attorney general once charged a defendant with the common-law offense of affray, arguing that the man committed the crime when he " 'arm[ed] himself with dangerous and unusual weapons, in such a manner as will naturally cause terror to the people.' " *Simpson v. State*, 13 Tenn. 356, 358 (1833). [The] Tennessee Supreme Court quashed the indictment, holding that the Statute of Northampton was never part of Tennessee law [and that if it had been,] the Tennessee Constitution's Second Amendment analogue had "completely abrogated it." [Other] state courts likewise recognized that the common law did not punish the carrying of deadly weapons *per se*, but only the carrying of such weapons "for the purpose of an affray, and in such manner as to strike terror to the people." *O'Neil* v. *State*, 16 Ala. 65 (1849). Therefore, those who sought to carry firearms publicly and peaceably in antebellum America were generally free to do so.

In the early to mid-19th century, some States began enacting laws that proscribed the concealed carry of pistols and other small weapons. As we recognized in *Heller*, "the majority of the 19th-century courts to consider the question held that [these] prohibitions on carrying concealed weapons were lawful under the Second Amendment or state analogues." [However], history reveals a consensus that States could *not* ban public carry altogether. Respondents' cited opinions agreed that concealed-carry prohibitions were constitutional only if they did not similarly prohibit *open* carry. [To be sure,] Tennessee's prohibition on carrying "publicly or privately" any "belt or pocket pisto[l]," 1821 Tenn. Acts ch. 13, p. 15, was, on its face, uniquely severe. That said, when the Tennessee Supreme Court addressed the constitutionality of a substantively identical successor provision, see 1870 Tenn. Acts ch. 13, § 1, p. 28, the court read this language to permit the public carry of larger, military-style pistols because any categorical prohibition on their carry would "violat[e] the constitutional right to keep arms." *Andrews v. State*, 50 Tenn. 165 (1871). [All] told, these antebellum state-court decisions evince a consensus view that States could not altogether prohibit the public carry of "arms" protected by the Second Amendment or state analogues.

[In] the mid-19th century, many jurisdictions began adopting surety statutes that required certain individuals to post bond before carrying weapons in public. Although respondents seize on these laws to justify the proper-cause restriction, their reliance on them is misplaced. These laws were not *bans* on public carry, and they typically targeted only those threatening to do harm. [While] New York presumes that individuals have *no* public carry right without a showing of heightened need, the surety statutes *presumed* that individuals had a right to public carry that could be burdened only if another could make out a specific showing of "reasonable cause to fear an injury, or breach of the peace." Mass. Rev. Stat., ch. 134, § 16 (1836). As William Rawle explained in an influential treatise, an individual's carrying of arms was "sufficient cause to require him to give surety of the peace" only when "attended with circumstances giving just reason to fear that he purposes to make an unlawful use of them." *A View of the Constitution of the United States of America* 126 (2d ed. 1829). [Thus], unlike New York's regime, a showing of special need was required only *after* an individual was reasonably accused of intending to injure another or breach the peace. And, even then, proving special need simply avoided a fee rather than a ban.

[To] summarize: The historical evidence from antebellum America does demonstrate that *the manner* of public carry was subject to reasonable regulation. Under the common law, individuals could not carry deadly weapons in a manner likely to terrorize others. Similarly, although surety statutes did not directly restrict public carry, they did provide financial incentives for responsible arms carrying. Finally, States could lawfully eliminate one kind of public carry—concealed carry—so long as they left open the option to carry openly. None of these historical limitations on the right to bear arms approach New York's proper-cause requirement because none operated to prevent law-abiding citizens with ordinary self-defense needs from carrying arms in public for that purpose.

4

Evidence from around the adoption of the Fourteenth Amendment also fails to support respondents' position. [Even] before the Civil War commenced in 1861, this Court indirectly affirmed the importance of the right to keep and bear arms in public. Writing for the Court in *Dred Scott v. Sandford* [Ch. 9, Sec. 2, I, infra], Chief Justice Taney offered what he thought was a parade of horribles that would result from recognizing that free blacks were citizens of the United States. If blacks were citizens, Taney fretted, they would be entitled to the privileges and immunities of citizens, including the right "to keep and carry arms *wherever they went*." (Emphasis added). Thus, even Chief Justice Taney recognized (albeit unenthusiastically in the case of blacks) that public carry was a component of the right to keep and bear arms—a right free blacks were often denied in antebellum America.

[In] 1868, Congress extended the 1866 Freedmen's Bureau Act and reaffirmed that freedmen were entitled to the "full and equal benefit of all

laws and proceedings concerning personal liberty [and] personal security
. . . *including the constitutional right to keep and bear arms*." (Emphasis
added). [Of] course, even during Reconstruction the right to keep and bear
arms had limits. But those limits were consistent with a right of the public
to peaceably carry handguns for self-defense. [As] for Reconstruction-era
state regulations, there was little innovation over the kinds of public-carry
restrictions that had been commonplace in the early 19th century. For
instance, South Carolina in 1870 authorized the arrest of "all who go armed
offensively, to the terror of the people," 1870 S. C. Acts p. 403, no. 288, § 4,
parroting earlier statutes that codified the common-law offense. That same
year, after it cleaved from Virginia, West Virginia enacted a surety statute
nearly identical to the one it inherited from Virginia. See W. Va. Code, ch.
153, § 8. Also in 1870, Tennessee essentially reenacted its 1821 prohibition
on the public carry of handguns but, as explained above, Tennessee courts
interpreted that statute to exempt large pistols suitable for military use.

Respondents and the United States, however, direct our attention
primarily to two late-19th-century cases in Texas. In 1871, Texas law
forbade anyone from "carrying on or about his person . . . any pistol . . .
unless he has reasonable grounds for fearing an unlawful attack on his
person." 1871 Tex. Gen. Laws § 1. The Texas Supreme Court upheld that
restriction in *English v. State*, 35 Tex. 473 (1871). [Four] years later, in
State v. Duke, 42 Tex. 455 (1875), the Texas Supreme Court [interpreted]
Texas' State Constitution to protect not only military-style weapons but
rather all arms "as are commonly kept, according to the customs of the
people, and are appropriate for open and manly use in self-defense."
[Nonetheless], after expanding the scope of firearms that warranted state
constitutional protection, *Duke* held that requiring any pistol-bearer to
have " 'reasonable grounds fearing an unlawful attack on [one's] person' "
was a "legitimate and highly proper" regulation of handgun carriage. [We]
acknowledge that the Texas cases support New York's proper-cause
requirement, which one can analogize to Texas' "reasonable grounds"
standard. But the Texas statute, and the rationales set forth in *English*
and *Duke*, are outliers. [The] Texas decisions therefore provide little
insight into how postbellum courts viewed the right to carry protected arms
in public. * * *

5

Finally, respondents point to the slight uptick in gun regulation during
the late-19th century—principally in the Western Territories. As we
suggested in *Heller*, however, late-19th-century evidence cannot provide
much insight into the meaning of the Second Amendment when it
contradicts earlier evidence.[28] [The] bare existence of these localized

---

[28] **[Ct's note]** We will not address any of the 20th-century historical evidence brought to bear
by respondents or their *amici*. As with their late-19th-century evidence, the 20th-century evidence

restrictions cannot overcome the overwhelming evidence of an otherwise enduring American tradition permitting public carry. [The] exceptional nature of these western restrictions is all the more apparent when one considers the miniscule territorial populations who would have lived under them. [These] western restrictions were irrelevant to more than 99% of the American population. [Further], because these territorial laws were rarely subject to judicial scrutiny, we do not know the basis of their perceived legality. [Finally], these territorial restrictions deserve little weight because they were—consistent with the transitory nature of territorial government—short lived. [They] appear more as passing regulatory efforts by not-yet-mature jurisdictions on the way to statehood, rather than part of an enduring American tradition of state regulation.

* * *

At the end of this long journey through the Anglo-American history of public carry, we conclude that respondents have not met their burden to identify an American tradition justifying the State's proper-cause requirement. The Second Amendment guaranteed to "all Americans" the right to bear commonly used arms in public subject to certain reasonable, well-defined restrictions. *Heller*. Those restrictions, for example, limited the intent for which one could carry arms, the manner by which one carried arms, or the exceptional circumstances under which one could not carry arms, such as before justices of the peace and other government officials. Apart from a few late-19th-century outlier jurisdictions, American governments simply have not broadly prohibited the public carry of commonly used firearms for personal defense. Nor, subject to a few late-in-time outliers, have American governments required law-abiding, responsible citizens to "demonstrate a special need for self-protection distinguishable from that of the general community" in order to carry arms in public.

The constitutional right to bear arms in public for self-defense is not "a second-class right, subject to an entirely different body of rules than the other Bill of Rights guarantees." *McDonald* (plurality opinion). We know of no other constitutional right that an individual may exercise only after demonstrating to government officers some special need. That is not how the First Amendment works when it comes to unpopular speech or the free exercise of religion. It is not how the Sixth Amendment works when it comes to a defendant's right to confront the witnesses against him. And it is not how the Second Amendment works when it comes to public carry for self-defense.

---

presented by respondents and their *amici* does not provide insight into the meaning of the Second Amendment when it contradicts earlier evidence.

New York's proper-cause requirement violates the Fourteenth Amendment in that it prevents law-abiding citizens with ordinary self-defense needs from exercising their right to keep and bear arms.

JUSTICE ALITO, concurring.

[Our] holding decides nothing about who may lawfully possess a firearm or the requirements that must be met to buy a gun. Nor does it decide anything about the kinds of weapons that people may possess. Nor have we disturbed anything that we said in *Heller* or *McDonald* about restrictions that may be imposed on the possession or carrying of guns. In light of what we have actually held, it is hard to see what legitimate purpose can possibly be served by most of the dissent's lengthy introductory section. Why, for example, does the dissent think it is relevant to recount the mass shootings that have occurred in recent years? Does the dissent think that laws like New York's prevent or deter such atrocities? Will a person bent on carrying out a mass shooting be stopped if he knows that it is illegal to carry a handgun outside the home? And how does the dissent account for the fact that one of the mass shootings near the top of its list took place in Buffalo? The New York law at issue in this case obviously did not stop that perpetrator. What is the relevance of statistics about the use of guns to commit suicide? Does the dissent think that a lot of people who possess guns in their homes will be stopped or deterred from shooting themselves if they cannot lawfully take them outside? The dissent cites statistics about the use of guns in domestic disputes, but it does not explain why these statistics are relevant to the question presented in this case. How many of the cases involving the use of a gun in a domestic dispute occur outside the home, and how many are prevented by laws like New York's? The dissent cites statistics on children and adolescents killed by guns, but what does this have to do with the question whether an adult who is licensed to possess a handgun may be prohibited from carrying it outside the home? Our decision, as noted, does not expand the categories of people who may lawfully possess a gun, and federal law generally forbids the possession of a handgun by a person who is under the age of 18, 18 U.S.C. §§ 922(x)(2)–(5), and bars the sale of a handgun to anyone under the age of 21, §§ 922(b)(1), (c)(1). [And] while the dissent seemingly thinks that the ubiquity of guns and our country's high level of gun violence provide reasons for sustaining the New York law, the dissent appears not to understand that it is these very facts that cause law-abiding citizens to feel the need to carry a gun for self-defense.

No one apparently knows how many of the 400 million privately held guns are in the hands of criminals, but there can be little doubt that many muggers and rapists are armed and are undeterred by the [New York] Law. Each year, the New York City Police Department (NYPD) confiscates thousands of guns, and it is fair to assume that the number of guns seized is a fraction of the total number held unlawfully. The police cannot disarm every person who acquires a gun for use in criminal activity; nor can they provide bodyguard protection for the State's nearly 20 million residents or the 8.8 million people who live in New York City. Some of these people live in high-crime neighborhoods. Some must traverse dark and dangerous streets in order to reach their homes after work or other evening activities. Some are members of groups whose members feel especially vulnerable. And some of these people reasonably believe that unless they can brandish or, if necessary, use a handgun in the case of attack, they may be murdered, raped, or suffer some other serious injury.

Ordinary citizens frequently use firearms to protect themselves from criminal attack. According to survey data, defensive firearm use occurs up to 2.5 million times per year. A Centers for Disease Control and Prevention report commissioned by former President Barack Obama reviewed the literature surrounding firearms use and noted that "[s]tudies that directly assessed the effect of actual defensive uses of guns ... have found consistently lower injury rates among gun-using crime victims compared with victims who used other self-protective strategies."

[The dissent complains] that the Court relies too heavily on history and should instead approve the sort of "means-end" analysis employed in this case by the Second Circuit. Under that approach, a court, in most cases, assesses a law's burden on the Second Amendment right and the strength of the State's interest in imposing the challenged restriction. This mode of analysis places no firm limits on the ability of judges to sustain any law restricting the possession or use of a gun. [Consider] the dissent filed in *Heller* by Justice Breyer, the author of today's dissent. At issue in *Heller* was an ordinance that made it impossible for any District of Columbia resident to keep a handgun in the home for self-defense. Even the respondent, who carried a gun on the job while protecting federal facilities, did not qualify. The District of Columbia law was an extreme outlier; only a few other jurisdictions in the entire country had similar laws. Nevertheless, Justice Breyer's dissent, while accepting for the sake of argument that the Second Amendment protects the right to keep a handgun in the home, concluded, based on essentially the same test that today's dissent defends, that the District's complete ban was constitutional. [Like] that dissent in *Heller*, the real thrust of today's dissent is that guns are bad and that States and local jurisdictions should be free to restrict them essentially as they see fit. That argument was rejected in *Heller*, [which] correctly recognized that the Second Amendment codifies the right of ordinary law-abiding Americans to protect themselves from lethal violence by possessing and, if necessary, using a gun.

In 1791, when the Second Amendment was adopted, there were no police departments, and many families lived alone on isolated farms or on the frontiers. If these people were attacked, they were on their own. It is hard to imagine the furor that would have erupted if the Federal

Government and the States had tried to take away the guns that these people needed for protection. Today, unfortunately, many Americans have good reason to fear that they will be victimized if they are unable to protect themselves. And today, no less than in 1791, the Second Amendment guarantees their right to do so.

JUSTICE KAVANAUGH, with whom THE CHIEF JUSTICE joins, concurring.

[The] Court's decision does not prohibit States from imposing licensing requirements for carrying a handgun for self-defense. In particular, the Court's decision does not affect the existing licensing regimes—known as "shall-issue" regimes—that are employed in 43 States. [New] York's outlier may-issue regime is constitutionally problematic because it grants open-ended discretion to licensing officials and authorizes licenses only for those applicants who can show some special need apart from self-defense. Those features of New York's regime—the unchanneled discretion for licensing officials and the special-need requirement—in effect deny the right to carry handguns for self-defense to many "ordinary, law-abiding citizens."

[Shall-issue] regimes may require a license applicant to undergo fingerprinting, a background check, a mental health records check, and training in firearms handling and in laws regarding the use of force, among other possible requirements. [The] 43 States that employ objective shall-issue licensing regimes for carrying handguns for self-defense may continue to do so. Likewise, the 6 States including New York potentially affected by today's decision may continue to require licenses for carrying handguns for self-defense so long as those States employ objective licensing requirements like those used by the 43 shall-issue States.

JUSTICE BARRETT, concurring.

[The] Court does not conclusively determine the manner and circumstances in which post-ratification practice may bear on the original meaning of the Constitution. Scholars have proposed competing and potentially conflicting frameworks for this analysis. [Relatedly], the Court avoids another "ongoing scholarly debate on whether courts should primarily rely on the prevailing understanding of an individual right when the Fourteenth Amendment was ratified in 1868" or when the Bill of Rights was ratified in 1791. Here, the lack of support for New York's law in either period makes it unnecessary to choose between them. But if 1791 is the benchmark, then New York's appeals to Reconstruction-era history would fail for the independent reason that this evidence is simply too late (in addition to too little). [So] today's decision should not be understood to endorse freewheeling reliance on historical practice from the mid-to-late 19th century to establish the original meaning of the Bill of Rights.

JUSTICE BREYER, with whom JUSTICE SOTOMAYOR and JUSTICE KAGAN join, dissenting.

In 2020, 45,222 Americans were killed by firearms. Since the start of this year (2022), there have been 277 reported mass shootings—an average of more than one per day. Gun violence has now surpassed motor vehicle crashes as the leading cause of death among children and adolescents. Many States have tried to address some of the dangers of gun violence just described by passing laws that limit, in various ways, who may purchase, carry, or use firearms of different kinds. The Court today severely burdens States' efforts to do so. It invokes the Second Amendment to strike down a New York law regulating the public carriage of concealed handguns.

[The] question before us concerns the extent to which the Second Amendment prevents democratically elected officials from enacting laws to address the serious problem of gun violence. And yet the Court today purports to answer that question without discussing the nature or severity of that problem.

In 2017, there were an estimated 393.3 million civilian-held firearms in the United States, or about 120 firearms per 100 people. That is more guns per capita than in any other country in the world. (By comparison, Yemen is second with about 52.8 firearms per 100 people—less than half the per capita rate in the United States—and some countries, like Indonesia and Japan, have fewer than one firearm per 100 people.)

Unsurprisingly, the United States also suffers a disproportionately high rate of firearm-related deaths and injuries. [In] 2015, approximately 36,000 people were killed by firearms nationwide. Of those deaths, 22,018 (or about 61%) were suicides, 13,463 (37%) were homicides, and 489 (1%) were unintentional injuries. On top of that, firearms caused an average of 85,694 emergency room visits for nonfatal injuries each year between 2009 and 2017.

Worse yet, gun violence appears to be on the rise. By 2020, the number of firearm-related deaths had risen to 45,222, or by about 25% since 2015. That means that, in 2020, an average of about 124 people died from gun violence every day. [And] the consequences of gun violence are borne disproportionately by communities of color, and Black communities in particular.

The dangers posed by firearms can take many forms. [Mass] shootings are just one part of the problem. Easy access to firearms can also make many other aspects of American life more dangerous. Consider, for example, the effect of guns on road rage. In 2021, an average of 44 people each month were shot and either killed or wounded in road rage incidents, double the annual average between 2016 and 2019. Some of those deaths might have been avoided if there had not been a loaded gun in the car.

The same could be said of protests: A study of 30,000 protests between January 2020 and June 2021 found that armed protests were nearly six times more likely to become violent or destructive than unarmed protests.

Or domestic disputes: Another study found that a woman is five times more likely to be killed by an abusive partner if that partner has access to a gun. Or suicides: A study found that men who own handguns are three times as likely to commit suicide than men who do not and women who own handguns are seven times as likely to commit suicide than women who do not.

Consider, too, interactions with police officers. The presence of a gun in the hands of a civilian poses a risk to both officers and civilians. [Prosecutors] and police chiefs tell us that most officers who are killed in the line of duty are killed by firearms; they explain that officers in States with high rates of gun ownership are three times as likely to be killed in the line of duty as officers in States with low rates of gun ownership. [They] also say that States with the highest rates of gun ownership report four times as many fatal shootings of civilians by police officers compared to States with the lowest rates of gun ownership.

These are just some examples of the dangers that firearms pose. There is, of course, another side to the story. I am not simply saying that "guns are bad." Some Americans use guns for legitimate purposes, such as sport (*e.g.*, hunting or target shooting), certain types of employment (*e.g.*, as a private security guard), or self-defense. Balancing these lawful uses against the dangers of firearms is primarily the responsibility of elected bodies, such as legislatures. It requires consideration of facts, statistics, expert opinions, predictive judgments, relevant values, and a host of other circumstances, which together make decisions about how, when, and where to regulate guns more appropriately legislative work. That consideration counsels modesty and restraint on the part of judges when they interpret and apply the Second Amendment.

[Justice] Alito asks why I have begun my opinion by reviewing some of the dangers and challenges posed by gun violence and what relevance that has to today's case. All of the above considerations illustrate that the question of firearm regulation presents a complex problem—one that should be solved by legislatures rather than courts. What kinds of firearm regulations should a State adopt? Different States might choose to answer that question differently. They may face different challenges because of their different geographic and demographic compositions. A State like New York, which must account for the roughly 8.5 million people living in the 303 square miles of New York City, might choose to adopt different (and stricter) firearms regulations than States like Montana or Wyoming, which do not contain any city remotely comparable in terms of population or density.

[The] question presented in this case concerns the extent to which the Second Amendment restricts different States (and the Federal Government) from working out solutions to these problems through democratic processes. The primary difference between the Court's view and mine is that I believe the Amendment allows States to take account of the serious problems posed by gun violence that I have just described. I fear that the Court's interpretation ignores these significant dangers and leaves States without the ability to address them.

[Without] an evidentiary record, there is no reason to assume that New York courts applying [the proper cause] standard fail to provide license applicants with meaningful review. And there is no evidentiary record to support the Court's assumption here. Based on the pleadings alone, we cannot know how often New York courts find the denial of a concealed-carry license to be arbitrary and capricious or on what basis.

[In addition,] the line between "may issue" and "shall issue" regimes is not as clear cut as the Court suggests, and that line depends at least in part on how statutory discretion is applied in practice. Here, because the Court strikes down New York's law without affording the State an opportunity to develop an evidentiary record, we do not know how much discretion licensing officers in New York have in practice or how that discretion is exercised, let alone how the licensing regimes in the other six "may issue" jurisdictions operate.

Even accepting the Court's line between "may issue" and "shall issue" regimes and assuming that its tally (7 "may issue" and 43 "shall issue" jurisdictions) is correct, that count does not support the Court's implicit suggestion that the seven "may issue" jurisdictions are somehow outliers or anomalies. The Court's count captures only a snapshot in time. [As] of 1987, 16 States and the District of Columbia prohibited concealed carriage outright, 26 States had "may issue" licensing regimes, 7 States had "shall issue" regimes, and 1 State (Vermont) allowed concealed carriage without a permit. Thus, it has only been in the last few decades that States have shifted toward "shall issue" licensing laws. Prior to that, most States operated "may issue" licensing regimes without legal or practical problem. Moreover, even considering, as the Court does, only the present state of play, its tally provides an incomplete picture because it accounts for only the number of States with "may issue" regimes, not the number of people governed by those regimes. By the Court's count, the seven "may issue" jurisdictions are New York, California, Hawaii, Maryland, Massachusetts, New Jersey, and the District of Columbia. Together, these seven jurisdictions comprise about 84.4 million people and account for over a quarter of the country's population.

And there are good reasons why these seven jurisdictions may have chosen not to follow other States in shifting toward "shall issue" regimes. The seven remaining "may issue" jurisdictions are among the most densely populated in the United States, [reflecting] in part the fact that these "may issue" jurisdictions contain some of the country's densest and most populous urban areas, *e.g.,* New York City, Los Angeles, San Francisco, the District of Columbia, Honolulu, and Boston. [Densely] populated urban areas face different kinds and degrees of dangers from gun violence than rural areas. It is thus easy to see why the seven "may issue" jurisdictions might choose to regulate firearm carriage more strictly than other States.

[New] York and its *amici* present substantial data justifying the State's decision to retain a "may issue" licensing regime. The data show that stricter gun regulations are associated with lower rates of firearm-related death and injury. [Justice] Alito points to competing empirical evidence that arrives at a different conclusion. But these types of disagreements are exactly the sort that are better addressed by legislatures than courts.

[The] *Heller* Court did not end its opinion with [its conclusion based on history]. After concluding that the Second Amendment protects an individual right to possess a firearm for self-defense, the *Heller* Court added that that right is "not unlimited." It thus had to determine whether the District of Columbia's law, which banned handgun possession in the home, was a permissible regulation of the right. In answering that second question, it said: "Under *any of the standards of scrutiny that we have applied to enumerated constitutional rights,* banning from the home 'the most preferred firearm in the nation to "keep" and use for protection of one's home and family' would fail constitutional muster." That language makes clear that the *Heller* Court understood some form of means-end scrutiny to apply. It did not need to specify whether that scrutiny should be intermediate or strict because, in its view, the District's handgun ban was so "severe" that it would have failed either level of scrutiny.

[The] Court today is wrong when it says that its rejection of means-end scrutiny and near-exclusive focus on history "accords with how we protect other constitutional rights." As the Court points out, we do look to history in the First Amendment context to determine "whether the expressive conduct falls outside of the category of protected speech." But, if conduct falls within a category of protected speech, we then use means-end scrutiny to determine whether a challenged regulation unconstitutionally burdens that speech. [Additionally], beyond the right to freedom of speech, we regularly use means-end scrutiny in cases involving other constitutional provisions. [Here the Court cited examples involving free exercise of religion, equal protection, and search or seizure limits.]

The upshot is that applying means-end scrutiny to laws that regulate the Second Amendment right to bear arms would not create a constitutional anomaly. Rather, it is the Court's rejection of means-end scrutiny and adoption of a rigid history-only approach that is anomalous.

The Court's near-exclusive reliance on history is not only unnecessary, it is deeply impractical. It imposes a task on the lower courts that judges cannot easily accomplish. Judges understand well how to weigh a law's objectives (its "ends") against the methods used to achieve those objectives (its "means"). Judges are far less accustomed to resolving difficult historical questions. Courts are, after all, staffed by lawyers, not historians. Legal experts typically have little experience answering contested historical questions or applying those answers to resolve contemporary problems.

[The majority offers] a laundry list of reasons to discount seemingly relevant historical evidence. The Court believes that some historical laws and decisions cannot justify upholding modern regulations because, it says, they were outliers. It explains that just two court decisions or three colonial laws are not enough to satisfy its test. But the Court does not say how many cases or laws would suffice "to show a tradition of public-carry regulation." Other laws are irrelevant, the Court claims, because they are too dissimilar from New York's concealed-carry licensing regime. But the Court does not say what "representative historical analogue," short of a "twin" or a "dead ringer," would suffice. Indeed, the Court offers many and varied reasons to reject potential representative analogues, but very few reasons to accept them. At best, the numerous justifications that the Court finds for rejecting historical evidence give judges ample tools to pick their friends out of history's crowd. At worst, they create a one-way ratchet that will disqualify virtually any "representative historical analogue" and make it nearly impossible to sustain common-sense regulations necessary to our Nation's safety and security.

[Even] under ideal conditions, historical evidence will often fail to provide clear answers to difficult questions. [Many] aspects of the history of firearms and their regulation are ambiguous, contradictory, or disputed. Unsurprisingly, the extent to which colonial statutes enacted over 200 years ago were actually enforced, the basis for an acquittal in a 17th-century decision, and the interpretation of English laws from the Middle Ages (to name just a few examples) are often less than clear. And even historical experts may reach conflicting conclusions based on the same sources.

[History may] be an especially inadequate tool when it comes to modern cases presenting modern problems. Consider the Court's apparent preference for founding-era regulation. Our country confronted profoundly different problems during that time period than it does today. [In] 1790, most of America's relatively small population of just four million people lived on farms or in small towns. Even New York City, the largest American city then, as it is now, had a population of just 33,000 people. Small founding-era towns are unlikely to have faced the same degrees and types of risks from gun violence as major metropolitan areas do today.

[Although] I hope—fervently—that future courts will be able to identify historical analogues supporting the validity of regulations that address new technologies, I fear that it will often prove difficult to identify analogous technological and social problems from Medieval England, the founding era, or the time period in which the Fourteenth Amendment was ratified. Laws addressing repeating crossbows, launcegays, dirks, dagges, skeines, stilladers, and other ancient weapons will be of little help to courts confronting modern problems.

[Indeed], the Court's application of its history-only test in this case demonstrates the very pitfalls described above. The historical evidence reveals a 700-year Anglo-American tradition of regulating the public carriage of firearms in general, and concealed or concealable firearms in particular. The Court spends more than half of its opinion trying to discredit this tradition. But, in my view, the robust evidence of such a tradition cannot be so easily explained away. Laws regulating the public carriage of weapons existed in England as early as the 13th century and on this Continent since before the founding. Similar laws remained on the books through the ratifications of the Second and Fourteenth Amendments through to the present day. Many of those historical regulations imposed significantly stricter restrictions on public carriage than New York's licensing requirements do today. Thus, even applying the Court's history-only analysis, New York's law must be upheld because "historical precedent from before, during, and ... after the founding evinces a comparable tradition of regulation." [The dissent next contested the majority's account of the historical materials from: A) England; B) the Colonies; C) the Founding Era; D) the 19th Century; and E) Postbellum Regulation.]

The Court disregards "20th-century historical evidence." But it is worth noting that the law the Court strikes down today is well over 100 years old, having been enacted in 1911 and amended to substantially its present form in 1913. That alone gives it a longer historical pedigree than at least three of the four types of firearms regulations that *Heller* identified as "presumptively lawful." [See] Carlton F.W. Larson, *Four Exceptions in Search of a Theory: District of Columbia v. Heller and Judicial Ipse Dixit*, 60 Hastings L.J. 1371 (2009) (concluding that "prohibitions on the possession of firearms by felons and the mentally ill [and] laws imposing conditions and qualifications on the commercial sale of arms" have their origins in the 20th century); *Kanter v. Barr*, 919 F.3d 437 (CA7 2019) (Barrett, J., dissenting) ("Founding-era legislatures did not strip felons of the right to bear arms simply because of their status as felons"). Like Justice Kavanaugh, I understand the Court's opinion today to cast no doubt on that aspect of *Heller*'s holding. But unlike Justice Kavanaugh, I find the disconnect between *Heller*'s treatment of laws prohibiting, for example, firearms possession by felons or the mentally ill, and the Court's treatment of New York's licensing regime, hard to square. The inconsistency suggests that the Court today takes either an unnecessarily cramped view of the relevant historical record or a needlessly rigid approach to analogical reasoning.

* * *

The historical examples of regulations similar to New York's licensing regime are legion. Closely analogous English laws were enacted beginning in the 13th century, and similar American regulations were passed during the colonial period, the founding era, the 19th century, and the 20th century. Not all of these laws were identical to New York's, but that is inevitable in an analysis that demands examination of seven centuries of history. At a minimum, the laws I have recounted *resembled* New York's law, similarly restricting the right to publicly carry weapons and serving roughly similar purposes. That is all that the Court's test, which allows and even encourages "analogical reasoning," purports to require.

[In] each instance, the Court finds a reason to discount the historical evidence's persuasive force. Some of the laws New York has identified are too old. But others are too recent. Still others did not last long enough. Some applied to too few people. Some were enacted for the wrong reasons. Some may have been based on a constitutional rationale that is now impossible to identify. Some arose in historically unique circumstances. And some are not sufficiently analogous to the licensing regime at issue here. But if the examples discussed above, taken together, do not show a tradition and history of regulation that supports the validity of New York's law, what could? Sadly, I do not know the answer to that question. What is worse, the Court appears to have no answer either.

[To] the extent that any uncertainty remains between the Court's view of the history and mine, that uncertainty counsels against relying on history alone. In my view, it is appropriate in such circumstances to look beyond the history and engage in what the Court calls means-end scrutiny. Courts must be permitted to consider the State's interest in preventing gun violence, the effectiveness of the contested law in achieving that interest, the degree to which the law burdens the Second Amendment right, and, if appropriate, any less restrictive alternatives. [New] York's Legislature considered the empirical evidence about gun violence and adopted a reasonable licensing law to regulate the concealed carriage of handguns in order to keep the people of New York safe. The Court today strikes down that law based only on the pleadings. It gives the State no opportunity to present evidence justifying its reasons for adopting the law or showing how the law actually operates in practice, and it does not so much as acknowledge these important considerations. Because I cannot agree with the Court's decision to strike New York's law down without allowing for discovery or the development of any evidentiary record, without considering the State's compelling interest in preventing gun violence and protecting the safety of its citizens, and without considering the potentially deadly consequences of its decision, I respectfully dissent.

NOTES AND QUESTIONS

1. ***When is means-end scrutiny appropriate?*** The dissent disagrees with the Court's characterization of its historical test as in accord with case law governing other constitutional rights. Even the majority apparently concedes that means-end scrutiny remains "appropriate" "elsewhere." Why? If a constitutional test that balances government interests against the exercise of the right to keep and bear arms gives insufficient weight to the latter, why would it be permissible with respect to other rights? Is it because the very decision to include constitutional protection for a right to keep and bear arms implies that the right outweighs any government interest in combating the inherent risks of firearms? Given that other rights carry inherent risks, can such a rationale be limited to the Second Amendment context?

2. ***Incorporation's implications.*** Following *McDonald*, *Timbs*, and *Ramos*, when the Fourteenth Amendment incorporates a provision of the Bill of Rights against state and local government, that right has the same content as it does against the federal government. Where a historical test applies, which history matters? As Justice Barrett observes in her concurrence, the Court does not decide how it would resolve a case in which evidence of the public meaning of a constitutional right points in different directions in 1791 (when the Bill of Rights was ratified) and 1868 (when the Fourteenth Amendment was ratified). If the issue arises, how should the Court resolve it? The argument for 1791 is straightforward: when the Fourteenth Amendment incorporated provisions of the Bill of Rights it incorporated by reference their original public meaning. Might there be a plausible competing argument for the 1868 understanding "updating" not only the meaning of a right against state and local action but federal action as well? Commentators sometimes refer to the process by which the Court has applied equal protection principles (which find expression in the Fourteenth Amendment but not the original Bill of Rights) to federal action as "reverse incorporation." See note 2(c) after *Bolling v. Sharpe*, Ch. 9, Sec. 2, II, infra. Is the notion that the Fourteenth Amendment could change the meaning of a provision of the Bill of Rights without altering the latter's text consistent with the interpretive premises of the *Bruen* majority? If not, does that call into question the application of equal protection limits against the federal government?

3. ***Assault weapons.*** Federal law forbids the sale of new machineguns, i.e., fully automatic firearms that can discharge multiple bullets with a single trigger pull. The *Heller* majority made clear (albeit in in dicta) that the ban is permissible because machineguns are not "typically possessed by law-abiding citizens for lawful purposes." What about semi-automatic weapons? Before *Bruen*, most courts rejected challenges to state and local restrictions on so-called assault weapons, typically defined by magazine capacity. *See, e.g., Kolbe v. Hogan*, 849 F.3d 114 (4thCir.2017); *Heller v. Dist. of Columbia*, 670 F.3d

1244 (D.C.Cir.2011). However, they did so using the means-end scrutiny that the *Bruen* majority rejects. Can such restrictions survive the *Bruen* historical test? Dissenting in the 2011 D.C. Circuit *Heller* case, then-Judge Kavanaugh substantially anticipated *Bruen*'s test and concluded that the District's ban on semi-automatic rifles was invalid under it, given that such weapons are in common use. Yet as he also observed, semi-automatic firearms did not exist before the first decade of the twentieth century. Thus, legislators and judges would have had no occasion to consider laws restricting them at the Founding or during Reconstruction. What sorts of regulations of what sorts of firearms in those periods provide the proper analogy for analyzing whether contemporary restrictions on large-capacity magazines fall within the historical tradition of permissible firearms regulation?

8. THE DEATH PENALTY AND RELATED PROBLEMS: CRUEL AND UNUSUAL PUNISHMENT

IV. ADDITIONAL CONSTITUTIONAL LIMITS ON IMPOSING SEVERE PUNISHMENT

P. 608, after the final paragraph:

In FORD v. WAINWRIGHT, 477 U.S. 399 (1986), the Supreme Court, per MARSHALL, J., held that the Eighth Amendment forbids executing a prisoner who has "lost his sanity" after sentencing. In MADISON v. ALABAMA, 139 S.Ct. 718 (2019), a 5–3 majority of the Court, per KAGAN, J., applied *Ford* in holding that a prisoner's mere failure to remember committing his crime does not preclude execution but dementia that renders him "unable to rationally understand the reasons for his sentence" does. The Court remanded for application of this standard. ALITO, J., joined by Thomas and Gorsuch, JJ., dissented on the grounds that only the memory question was properly before the Court and that, in any event, the state court had applied the correct standard to the dementia question.

P. 611, after the first full paragraph:

In JONES v. MISSISSIPPI, 141 S.Ct. 1307 (2021), KAVANAUGH, J., in an opinion for the Court, concluded that a juvenile's sentence of LWOP complies with *Miller* so long as the judge acknowledges discretion to impose a lesser sentence, even without making a factual finding that the defendant is permanently incorrigible. SOTOMAYOR, J., joined by Breyer and Kagan, JJ., dissented, arguing that the majority's ruling failed to honor *Miller*'s requirement that a sentencing court offer an individualized reason to conclude that the particular defendant lacks the "distinctive attributes of youth [that] diminish the penological justifications for imposing the harshest sentences on juvenile offenders, even when they commit terrible crimes."

P. 614, before Section 9:

In BUCKLEW v. PRECYTHE, 139 S.Ct. 1112 (2019), a prisoner argued that Missouri's one-drug protocol would be unconstitutional as applied to him because vascular tumors in his head, neck, and throat posed a substantial risk of excruciating pain during the execution. GORSUCH, J., writing for a 5–4 Court, rejected the claim on the ground that in as-applied no less than facial challenges to a method of execution the challenger bears the burden of identifying a " 'feasible, readily implemented' alternative procedure that would 'significantly reduce a substantial risk of severe pain' " (quoting *Glossip* plurality opinion). According to the majority, execution by nitrogen hypoxia, the alternative method to which the prisoner eventually pointed, did not satisfy this standard. BREYER, J., joined by Ginsburg, Sotomayor, and Kagan, JJ., dissented on multiple grounds, including the contention that as-applied challenges should be treated differently from facial ones because the former do not undercut any legislative judgment: "It is impossible to believe that Missouri's legislature, when adopting lethal injection, considered the possibility that it would cause prisoners to choke on their own blood for up to several minutes before they die."

CHAPTER 7

FREEDOM OF EXPRESSION AND ASSOCIATION

■ ■ ■

1. THE SCOPE AND STRENGTH OF THE FIRST AMENDMENT

I. ADVOCACY OF ILLEGAL ACTION

D. A Modern "Restatement"

P. 680, at end of note 8:

In NIEVES v. BARTLETT, 139 S.Ct. 1715 (2019), the Court seemingly narrowed its conclusion in *Lozman*. In *Nieves*, Russell Bartlett had been arrested for disorderly conduct and resisting arrest in the context of an altercation that took place during an Alaska sports festival "known for both extreme sports and extreme alcohol consumption." The criminal charges against Bartlett were ultimately dismissed, whereupon he sued the arresting officers, including Nieves, under 42 U.S.C. § 1983, claiming that his arrest was in retaliation for his speech, in particular his comments during the altercation about the behavior of the arresting officers. The district court having determined that the officers had probable cause to arrest Bartlett, the issue then turned on the question of the burden of proof in a retaliatory arrest claim based on an allegation that the arrest was in retaliation for engaging in otherwise protected speech.

Writing for the Court, ROBERTS, C.J., noted that *Lozman* was based on "unusual circumstances" and that *Nieves v. Bartlett* presented a "more representative case." And in this more representative case, the Court concluded that the plaintiff must establish a causal connection between the impermissible retaliatory motive and the subsequent arrest, and that the causal connection must be of the "but for" variety. Noting that "protected speech is often a legitimate consideration when deciding whether to make an arrest," the Court concluded that the presence of probable cause would generally (*Lozman* presenting the narrow exception of the presence of probable cause under circumstances in which it could objectively be shown that otherwise similarly situated individuals not engaged in protected speech would not have been arrested) defeat a retaliatory arrest claim. When there was no probable cause for the arrest, it would still be necessary for the plaintiff to show that the retaliation was a "substantial or motivating factor behind the arrest." If a plaintiff were able to make such a showing, then the burden of proof would shift to the defendant to show that the arrest would have been initiated without respect to the retaliation.

THOMAS, J., concurring in part and concurring in the judgment, would have rejected even the *Lozman* exception. GORSUCH, J., concurring in part and dissenting in part, stressed that for him the presence of probable cause was relevant to a retaliatory arrest claim, but that it was not nearly as conclusive as it appeared to be for the majority. GINSBURG, J., concurring in part and dissenting in part, also objected to the weight given by the majority to the presence of probable cause. And SOTOMAYOR, J., dissenting, also took issue with the almost conclusive role the majority gave to the presence of probable cause, believing, with Ginsburg, J., that the proper approach was one drawn from *Mt. Healthy City Bd. of Educ. v. Doyle*, 429 U.S. 274 (1977), in which "the plaintiff bears the burden of demonstrating that unconstitutional animus was a motivating factor for an adverse action; the burden then shifts to the defendant to demonstrate that, even without any impetus to retaliate, the defendant would have taken the action complained of."

As both *Lozman* and *Nieves* exemplify, First Amendment retaliation claims have become increasingly common, with claimants arguing that otherwise permissible government restrictions or other negative actions have been impermissibly motivated by the claimant's constitutionally protected speech. In HOUSTON COMMUNITY COLLEGE SYSTEM v. WILSON, 142 S.Ct. 1253 (2022), however, a unanimous Court again emphasized the limits of retaliation claims.

Wilson, an elected member of the governing board of the Houston Community College System, had long been a gadfly, frequently suing the board and its members and even more often engaging in intemperate public criticism of the board, its policies, and its members. In response, the board publicly censured Wilson, an action that entailed no tangible consequences other than ineligibility to hold certain board offices. Wilson challenged the censure on First Amendment grounds, arguing that the censure itself was impermissible retaliation for engaging in constitutionally protected public political speech, and thus in violation of the First Amendment. The case came before the Court in a complex procedural posture, the result of which was that the only question before the Court was whether a "purely verbal censure," unaccompanied by any other "material adverse action," could ground a First Amendment retaliation claim in the context of a public elected body.

Writing for a unanimous Court, GORSUCH, J., rejected Wilson's claim. Relying heavily on the history of legislative and related censures, and on the fact of legislative censure being a "long settled and established practice," the Court concluded that purely verbal censure of one of its members by an elected assembly could not provide the basis for a First Amendment retaliation claim. Moreover, the Court relied not only on the fact that legislative censure of one of its members had a lengthy history, but also on the way in which the censure itself might be understood as First Amendment activity by the censuring body.

Moreover, being susceptible to public criticism, the Court pointed out, is an aspect of serving on a public body. All of these considerations combined to lead to the unanimous rejection of Wilson's argument, at least in the context of an elected public body and at least in the context of the absence of any "material adverse action" other than the censure itself, a conclusion from which there were no dissenting views.

II. REPUTATION AND PRIVACY

B. Public Officials and Seditious Libel

P. 696, add as new note 6 after note 5:

6. *Challenging New York Times.* In an era of social media, enhanced forms of electronic transmission, and the seeming accelerating proliferation of factual falsity, including demonstrable falsehoods about specific individuals, calls to reconsider *New York Times* have increased. On the desirability of fine-tuning around the edges in light of contemporary issues and technology, see David Logan, *Rescuing Our Democracy by Rethinking* New York Times v. Sullivan, 81 Ohio St. L.J. 759 (2020); Cass R. Sunstein, *Falsehoods and the First Amendment*, 33 Harv. J.L. & Tech. 388 (2020). And in opinions at the end of the 2020 Term dissenting from denials of certiorari in *Berisha v. Lawson*, 141 S.Ct. 2424 (2021), Justices Thomas and Gorsuch, in separate opinions, urged more substantial reconsideration of *New York Times*. Justice Thomas, echoing his earlier dissenting opinion in *McKee v. Cosby*, 139 S.Ct. 675 (2019) (Thomas, J., dissenting from the denial of certiorari), decried the full development of *New York Times v. Sullivan* and its progeny as departing from the historical understanding of the First Amendment and urged, more specifically, that its extension to public figures as well as public officials was especially problematic. And Justice Gorsuch, noting occasional academic questions about *New York Times* (including from then-Professor Elena Kagan), called for reconsideration in light of the "real harm" that falsehoods about specific individuals could inflict and in light of the vast changes wrought by modern political and technological developments.

Even more recently, in *Coral Ridge Ministries Media, Inc. v. Southern Poverty Law Center*, 142 S.Ct. 2453 (2022), Justice Thomas, again in the context of dissenting from a denial of certiorari, continued to urge that that the "actual malice" standard from *New York Times* be reconsidered. The underlying litigation was a libel action by Coral Ridge against the Southern Poverty Law Center for having publicly labeled Coral Ridge an "anti-LGBT hate group," resulting in Coral Ridge's exclusion from various fund-raising opportunities. The courts below found liability to have been precluded by *New York Times*, a result that Justice Thomas argued illustrated the need for reconsideration.

2. THE PROBLEM OF CONTENT REGULATION

P. 833, at the end of note 3:

Two Terms after *Matal v. Tam*, the Court revisited the issue of offensive trademarks in IANCU v. BRUNETTI, 139 S.Ct. 2294 (2019), where the Court held that the Lanham Act's prohibition on registration for "immoral or scandalous" trademarks constituted impermissible viewpoint-based discrimination. At issue was an attempted registration of the trademark FUCT by the clothing manufacturer who used these four letters, allegedly pronounced as four separate letters, as the brand name for its clothing line. Relying substantially on *Matal*, the Court, with KAGAN, J., writing the majority opinion, rejected the argument that the "immoral or scandalous" standard was merely a viewpoint-neutral restriction on the manner in which a point of view could be expressed but was not itself a viewpoint-based standard. The Court also rejected the government's argument that the statutory criteria were not facially invalid but only that there had been errors in application by trademark examiners in applying the criteria, and rejected as well the argument that the statute could be subject to a saving narrowing construction.

Concurring, ALITO, J., noted that a redrafted statute precluding registration of "vulgar terms" could likely be valid, but that "[v]iewpoint discrimination is poison to a free society. But in many countries with constitutions or legal traditions that claim to protect freedom of speech, serious viewpoint discrimination is now tolerated, and such discrimination has become increasingly prevalent in this country. At a time when free speech is under attack, it is especially important for this Court to remain firm on the principle that the First Amendment does not tolerate viewpoint discrimination."

ROBERTS, C.J., BREYER, J., and SOTOMAYOR, J., each wrote opinions concurring in part and dissenting in part. All three agreed with the majority that the "immoral" component in the statutory standard was impermissibly viewpoint-based, but that it could be excised by the Court, leaving the "scandalous" element in place, an element that for all three of these concurring justices was sufficiently close a restriction on only the lewd or the profane that it could be understood as not being viewpoint-based. Justice Breyer's opinion also objected to the Court's continuing reliance on rigid First Amendment categories, believing that the Court should focus on the "more basic proportionality question" whether the harm to the First Amendment's interests was disproportionate to the government's regulatory objectives.

I. "HATE SPEECH" AND THE *SKOKIE* CONTROVERSY

P. 882, after *Reed v. Gilbert*:

————

The Court's divisions over the scope and strength of the bar against content regulation have continued. BARR v. AMERICAN ASSOCIATION

OF POLITICAL CONSULTANTS, INC., 140 S.Ct. 2335 (2020), produced a decision whose lack of a majority opinion underscored the way in which content regulation doctrine remains in flux and contested.

The case concerned the Telephone Consumer Protection Act of 1991, which in relevant part prohibits virtually all robocalls to cell phones. In 2015, however, Congress amended the Act to exclude from the robocall prohibition calls made to collect a government debt, a category including many student loans and home mortgages. An association of political consultants, many of whose members wished to be able to make political robocalls to cell phones, challenged the amended Act, arguing that its preference for government debt-collection robocalls over political robocalls violated the First Amendment.

In a fractured set of opinions, the Court agreed that the amended Act engaged in constitutionally impermissible content discrimination in violation of the First Amendment, and that the appropriate remedy, affirming the Fourth Circuit decision below, was to sever the constitutionally flawed government debt exception, leaving the overall robocall prohibition, without the exception, in place.

KAVANAUGH, J., writing for a plurality including himself, Roberts, C.J. Thomas, J. (in part), and Alito, J., relied heavily on *Reed* in concluding that the exception for government debt collection "impermissibly favored [government] debt-collection speech over political and other speech," and thus constituted unconstitutional content discrimination. Emphasizing that "content-based laws are subject to strict scrutiny," Justice Kavanaugh reiterated *Reed*'s conclusion that strict scrutiny applied to laws that "single[ ] out specific subject matter for differential treatment." For the plurality, the fact that the regulation was part of a broader regulatory scheme regulating the economic activity of debt collection was of no moment, because here the regulation of speech was not merely incidental to a broader regulatory program. Quoting *Sorrell v. IMS*, *supra*, Justice Kavanaugh argued that "the law here ['does] not simply have an effect on speech, but is directed at certain content and is aimed at particular speakers' "

Having concluded that strict scrutiny was the applicable standard, the merits of the controversy were essentially over, with even the government having conceded that "collecting government debt" was not the kind of interest that would satisfy strict scrutiny. But the question remained about the remedy. For the plurality, traditional severability principles were applicable, the most important of which, in this context, was the "presumption of severability." Applying that presumption and finding that the robocall prohibition without the government debt collection exception was "capable of functioning independently," *Murphy v. National Collegiate Athletic Association*, 138 S.Ct. 1461 (2018), the plurality held the unconstitutional exception severable, leaving the original exception-less robocall prohibition in place.

Much of the cause of the lack of a majority opinion was the issue of severability. GORSUCH, J., joined in part by Thomas, J., agreed with some of the plurality's analysis of the merits of the case but disagreed about severability. For Justice Gorsuch, the basic prohibition on robocalls to cell phones was itself an impermissible form of content regulation. As a result, he argued, severing the exception did not cure the basic problem, and he would have invalidated the entire prohibition. SOTOMAYOR, J., disagreed with the majority's content regulation analysis but concurred in the judgment because she agreed that the offending provision, if unconstitutional, was severable. BREYER, J., joined by Ginsburg and Kagan, JJ., reiterated his continuing concern with treating content regulation in almost all of its forms as triggering strict scrutiny. Although he consequently disagreed with the majority's view about the merits, he concurred in the judgment because he agreed that a provision that a majority of the Court had found constitutionally objectionable was severable from the entire statute.

The scope and strength of *Reed* continued to be an issue in the 2021 Term, with indications that *Reed*'s broad condemnation of most content-based distinctions was not as broad or strong as some had feared. In CITY OF AUSTIN v. REAGAN NATIONAL ADVERTISING, 142 S.Ct. 1464 (2022), the question was whether a municipality could impose different and greater restrictions on advertising using "off-premises" billboards, signs, and the like than it imposed on signs located on the premises of the establishment the signs were advertising. Such distinctions between on-premises and off-premises advertising signs are widespread (cf. *Railway Express Agency v. New York* (1949, Ch. 9, Sec.1 infra), but were challenged here on the grounds that they constituted impermissible content-based discrimination under *Reed*. The particular issue was a restriction on certain digitally controllable and changeable electronic signs, a restriction imposed in the name of aesthetics and safety on off-premises signs but not on on-premises signs.

The challengers argued, relying on *Reed*, that the distinction was content-based and demanded strict scrutiny, but the Court, with SOTOMAYOR, J., writing the majority opinion, concluded that the distinction here "require[d] an examination of [the content of] speech only in service of drawing neutral, location-based lines. [The locational distinction] is agnostic as to content. Thus, absent a content-based purpose or justification, the City's distinction is content neutral and does not warrant the application of strict scrutiny."

The Court in *Austin* distinguished *Reed* by observing that the Austin distinction was not based on topic or subject matter. "A given sign is treated differently based solely on whether it is located on the same premises as the thing being discussed or not. The message on the sign matters only to the extent that it informs the sign's relative location. The on-/off-premises distinction is therefore similar to ordinary time, place, or manner restrictions." "Underlying [our previous cases] is a rejection of the view that *any* examination of speech or expression inherently triggers heightened First Amendment concern. Rather, it is [only] regulations that discriminate based on 'the topic discussed or the idea or message expressed' that are content based. *Reed*."

In a concurring opinion, BREYER, J., acknowledged that *Reed* was "binding precedent," but reiterated his view that *Reed* was wrongly decided. "[T]he First Amendment is not the Tax Code. Its purposes are often better served when judge-made categories (like 'content discrimination') are treated, not as bright-line rules, but instead as rules of thumb. [Many] ordinary regulatory programs may well turn on the content of speech without posing any 'realistic possibility [of] official suppression of ideas'."

ALITO, J., concurring in the judgment and dissenting in part, offered examples of signs that might render Austin's on-premises/off-premises distinction more problematic, and thus concluded that the Court should have held the particular provisions at issue "not facially unconstitutional" and said nothing more. THOMAS, J., joined by Gorsuch, J., and Barrett, J., dissented, arguing that *Reed* was controlling and that any distinction requiring reference to the communicative content of a sign, including reference to content in determining whether the sign was on-premises or off-premises, represented a content-based distinction requiring strict scrutiny. Justice Thomas argued further that the only prior decision supporting the majority's understanding of content-neutral locational restrictions was *Hill v. Colorado* (Sec. 3, II infra), which he insisted was widely understood to have been wrongly decided in holding that its locational restriction on abortion protests was not content-based.

4. NEW CATEGORIES?

I. HARM TO CHILDREN AND THE OVERBREADTH DOCTRINE

P. 923, add as new final paragraph to note 4:

Overbreadth doctrine remains both contested and misunderstood. In *Americans for Prosperity Foundation v. Bonta*, 141 S.Ct. 2373 (2021), discussed at length, *infra*, addition to p. 1162, the majority characterized as an overbreadth challenge what others would see simply as a facial challenge. Is a facial challenge, which, if successful, invalidates a statute in all of its applications, the same as an overbreadth challenge, as Roberts, C.J. seems to conclude in *Americans for Prosperity*, or is overbreadth merely a First-Amendment-specific standing doctrine applicable when a particular challenger who is not engaged in protected conduct challenges statute because it reaches the unprotected conduct of others?

7. GOVERNMENT SPEECH

I. SUBSIDIES OF SPEECH

P. 1063, add after Walker:

———

As in *Walker*, the question whether a government enterprise involving citizen participation was government speech, or, instead, a public forum, was the issue in SHURTLEFF v. CITY OF BOSTON, 142 S.Ct. 1583 (2022). For years, the City of Boston had permitted private organizations to raise their flags for a limited period of time on one of the three flagpoles in the plaza in front of Boston City Hall. Although one of the flagpoles was reserved by the city for the American flag and a second for the flag of the Commonwealth of Massachusetts, the city had routinely allowed various groups to raise that group's flag on the third flagpole. Some of these flag raisings were by foreign countries whose officials were visiting Boston, some were by various organizations seeking to commemorate this or that social or political cause, and some were even by private corporations seeking to advertise their products and services. But when Shurtleff, director of an organization called Camp Constitution, sought to hold a flagraising event to "commemorate the civil and social contributions of the Christian community," the city turned him down, relying heavily on what it perceived to be the constraints of the Establishment Clause of the First Amendment in prohibiting, Boston believed, official endorsements of religion.

The issues paralleled those in *Walker*, and, earlier, *Summum*. Shurtleff claimed that the flagraising opportunity was some form of public forum, or at least private speech, such that excluding him and his organization constituted impermissible content discrimination. But Boston argued both that allowing the overtly religious flag would have created Establishment Clause problems and that choosing which flags to display on its flagpoles on its property was government speech unconstrained, even as to viewpoint, by the First Amendment.

Relying on the fact that Boston had never before denied a flagraising request by a private group, and on *Matal v. Tam* (2017, Sec. 2 supra), a unanimous Court sided with Shurtleff and rejected Boston's government speech argument. Writing for the Court, BREYER, J., acknowledged that the line between government speech and private expression "can blur when, as here, a government invites the people to participate in the program." But applying a contextual and "holistic" inquiry, and emphasizing the City's historical approval without scrutiny of all flagraising applications, the Court concluded that that this was not government speech. "[W]hile the historical practice of flag flying at government buildings favors Boston, the city's lack of meaningful involvement in the selection of flags or the crafting of their messages leads us to classify the flag raisings as private, not government, speech—though nothing prevents Boston from changing its policies going forward."

Having rejected Boston's government speech claim, the Court quickly and easily found this to be a case of impermissible viewpoint discrimination. "When a government does not speak for itself, it may not exclude speech based on 'religious viewpoint'; doing so 'constitutes impermissible viewpoint discrimination.' *Good News Club v. Milford Central School* (2001, Sec. 3, fn 132 supra; Ch. 8, III, Sec. 1 infra)."

KAVANAUGH, J., filed a concurring opinion, emphasizing that "a government does not violate the Establishment Clause because it treats religious persons, organizations, and speech equally with secular persons, organizations, and speech in public programs, benefits, facilities, and the like [see *Capitol Square Review & Advisory Board v. Pinette*, 1995, Ch. 8, Sec. 1 infra]. On the contrary, a government *violates* the Constitution when (as here) it *excludes* religious persons, organizations, or speech because of religion from public programs, benefits, facilities, and the like."

ALITO, J., joined by Thomas, J, and Gorsuch, J., concurred in the judgment. Repeating the concerns he expressed in *Walker*, he worried that government speech doctrine could too easily or too often be used as a "cover for censorship." To prevent this, he argued, the focus must be on the identity of the speaker. Rejecting the approach of *Walker* and of the majority here, he insisted that "government speech occurs if—but only if— a government purposefully expresses a message of its own through persons authorized to speak on its behalf, and in doing so, does not rely on a means that abridges private speech. [Government] speech is thus the purposeful communication of a governmentally determined message by a person exercising a power to speak for a government."

GORSUCH, J., joined by Thomas, J., also concurred in the judgment only, writing at length to dismiss Boston's Establishment Clause argument, and laying the blame at the feet of *Lemon v. Kurtzman* (1971, Ch. 8, II, Sec. 1 infra), a case essentially overruled by *Kennedy v. Bremerton School District*, 142 S.Ct. 2407 (2022) (this Supplement, Ch. 8, infra).

II. GOVERNMENT AS EDUCATOR AND EDITOR

P. 1094, remove note 4 and add after note 3:

MAHANOY AREA SCHOOL DISTRICT V. B. L.

594 U.S. ___, 141 S.Ct. 2038, 210 L.Ed.2d 403 (2021).

JUSTICE BREYER delivered the opinion of the Court.

A public high school student used, and transmitted to her Snapchat friends, vulgar language and gestures criticizing both the school and the school's cheerleading team. The student's speech took place outside of school hours and away from the school's campus. In response, the school suspended the student for a year from the cheerleading team. We must decide whether [the] school's decision violated the First Amendment. Although we do not agree with the reasoning of the Third Circuit panel's majority, we do agree with its conclusion that the school's disciplinary action violated the First Amendment.

B. L. was a student at Mahanoy Area High School in Mahanoy City, Pennsylvania. At the end of her freshman year, B. L. tried out for a position on the school's varsity cheerleading squad. [She] did not make the varsity cheerleading team [but] was offered a spot on the cheerleading squad's junior varsity team. B. L. did not accept the coach's decision with good grace, particularly because the squad coaches had placed an entering freshman on the varsity team.

That weekend, B. L. and a friend visited [a] local convenience store. There, B. L. used her smartphone to post two photos on Snapchat, a social media application that allows users to post photos and videos that disappear after a set period of time. B. L. posted the images to her Snapchat "story," a feature of the application that allows any person in the user's "friend" group (B. L. had about 250 "friends") to view the images for a 24 hour period. The first image B. L. posted showed B. L. and a friend with middle fingers raised; it bore the caption: "Fuck school fuck softball fuck cheer fuck everything." The second image was blank but for a caption, which read: "Love how me and [another student] get told we need a year of jv before we make varsity but tha[t] doesn't matter to anyone else?" The caption also contained an upside-down smiley-face emoji.

B. L.'s Snapchat "friends" included other Mahanoy Area High School students, some of whom also belonged to the cheerleading squad. At least one of them, using a separate cellphone, took pictures of B. L.'s posts and shared them with other members of the cheerleading squad. One of the students who received these photos showed them to her mother (who was a cheerleading squad coach), and the images spread. That week, several cheerleaders and other students approached the cheerleading coaches "visibly upset" about B. L.'s posts. Questions about the posts persisted during an Algebra class taught by one of the two coaches. After discussing the matter with the school principal, the coaches decided that because the posts used profanity in connection with a school extracurricular activity, they violated team and school rules. As a result, the coaches suspended B. L. from the junior varsity cheerleading squad for the upcoming year. B. L.'s subsequent apologies did not move school officials. The school's athletic director, principal, superintendent, and school board all affirmed B. L.'s suspension from the team. In response, B. L., with her parents, filed this lawsuit in Federal District Court.

The District Court found in B. L.'s favor, [finding] that B. L.'s Snapchats had not caused substantial disruption at the school. [The] District Court declared that B. L.'s punishment violated the First Amendment, awarded B. L. nominal damages and attorneys' fees, and ordered the school to expunge her disciplinary record. On appeal, a panel of the Third Circuit affirmed. [The] majority noted that *Tinker* [held] that a public high school could not constitutionally prohibit a peaceful student political demonstration consisting of " 'pure speech' " on school property during the school day. In *Tinker*, this Court emphasized that there was no evidence the student protest would "substantially interfere with the work of the school or impinge upon the rights of other students." . . .

Many courts have taken this statement as setting a standard [that] allows schools considerable freedom on campus to discipline students for conduct that the First Amendment might otherwise protect. But here, the panel majority held that this additional freedom did "not apply to off-campus speech," which it defined as "speech that is outside school-owned, -operated, or -supervised channels and that is not reasonably interpreted as bearing the school's imprimatur." Because B. L.'s speech took place off campus, the panel concluded that [*Tinker*] did not apply and the school consequently could not discipline B. L. for engaging in a form of pure speech.

[We] have made clear that students do not "shed their constitutional rights to freedom of speech or expression," even "at the school house gate." But we have also made clear that courts must apply the First Amendment "in light of the special characteristics of the school environment." One such characteristic [is] that schools at times stand *in loco parentis*, *i.e.*, in the place of parents. This Court has [outlined] three specific categories of student speech that schools may regulate in certain circumstances: (1) "indecent," "lewd," or "vulgar" speech uttered during a school assembly on school grounds. *Bethel*. (2) speech, uttered during a class trip, that promotes "illegal drug use," *Morse* v. *Frederick*; and (3) speech that others may reasonably perceive as "bear[ing] the imprimatur of the school," [as] in a school-sponsored newspaper, *Kuhlmeier*. Finally, in *Tinker*, we said schools have a special interest in regulating speech that "materially disrupts classwork or involves substantial disorder or invasion of the rights of others."

Unlike the Third Circuit, we do not believe the special characteristics that give schools additional license to regulate student speech always disappear when a school regulates speech that takes place off campus. The school's regulatory interests remain significant in some off-campus circumstances. [These] include serious or severe bullying or harassment targeting particular individuals; threats aimed at teachers or other students; the failure to follow rules concerning lessons, the writing of papers, the use of computers, or participation in other online school activities; and breaches of school security devices, including material maintained within school computers.

Even B. L. herself and the *amici* supporting her would redefine the Third Circuit's off-campus/on-campus distinction, treating as on campus: all times when the school is responsible for the student; the school's immediate surroundings; travel en route to and from the school; all speech taking place over school laptops or on a school's website; speech taking place during remote learning; activities taken for school credit; and communications to school e-mail accounts or phones. And it may be that speech related to extracurricular activities, such as team sports, would also receive special treatment under B. L.'s proposed rule.

We are uncertain as to the length or content of any such list of appropriate exceptions or carveouts to the Third Circuit majority's rule. [Particularly] given the advent of computer-based learning, we hesitate to determine precisely which of many school-related off-campus activities belong on such a list. Neither do we now know how such a list might vary, depending upon a student's age, the nature of the school's off-campus activity, or the impact upon the school itself. Thus, we do not now set forth a broad, highly general First Amendment rule stating just what counts as "off campus" speech and whether or how ordinary First Amendment standards must give way off campus to a school's special need to prevent, *e.g.,* substantial disruption of learning-related activities or the protection of those who make up a school community.

We can, however, mention three features of off-campus speech that [distinguish] schools' efforts to regulate that speech from their efforts to regulate on-campus speech. [*First,*] a school, in relation to off-campus speech, will rarely stand *in loco parentis.* The doctrine of *in loco parentis* treats school administrators as standing in the place of students' parents under circumstances where the children's actual parents cannot protect, guide, and discipline them. Geographically speaking, off-campus speech will normally fall within the zone of parental, rather than school-related, responsibility. *Second,* from the student speaker's perspective, regulations of off-campus speech, when coupled with regulations of on-campus speech, include all the speech a student utters during the full 24-hour day. That means courts must be more skeptical of a school's efforts to regulate off-campus speech, for doing so may mean the student cannot engage in that kind of speech at all. When it comes to political or religious speech that occurs outside school or a school program or activity, the school will have a heavy burden to justify intervention. *Third*, the school itself has an interest in protecting a student's unpopular expression, especially when the expression takes place off campus. America's public schools are the nurseries of democracy. . . .

Given the many different kinds of off-campus speech, [we] can [say] little more than this: Taken together, these three features of much off-campus speech mean that the leeway the First Amendment grants to schools [is] diminished. We leave for future cases to decide where, when, and how these features mean the speaker's off-campus location will make the critical difference. This case can, however, provide one example. [Putting] aside the vulgar language, the listener would hear criticism of the team, the team's coaches, and the school—[i.e., criticism] of the rules of a community of which B. L. forms a part. This criticism did not involve features that place it outside the First Amendment's ordinary protection. B. L.'s posts, while crude, did not amount to fighting words. And while B. L. used vulgarity, her speech was not obscene as this Court has understood that term. To the contrary, B. L. uttered the kind of pure speech to which, were she an adult, the First Amendment would provide strong protection.

Consider too when, where, and how B. L. spoke. Her posts appeared outside of school hours from a location outside the school. She did not identify the school in her posts or target any member of the school community with vulgar or abusive language. B. L. also transmitted her speech through a personal cellphone, to an audience consisting of her private circle of Snapchat friends. These features of her speech, while risking transmission to the school itself, nonetheless diminish the school's interest in punishing B. L.'s utterance.

But what about the school's interest [in] prohibiting students from using vulgar language to criticize a school team or its coaches—at least when that criticism might well be transmitted to other students, team members, coaches, and faculty? We can break that general interest into three parts.

First, we consider the school's interest in teaching good manners and consequently in punishing the use of vulgar language aimed at part of the school community. The strength of this anti-vulgarity interest is weakened considerably by the fact that B. L. spoke outside the school on her own time. B. L. spoke under circumstances where the school did not stand *in loco parentis*. And there is no reason to believe B. L.'s parents had delegated to school officials their own control of B. L.'s behavior at the [convenience store]. Moreover, the vulgarity in B. L.'s posts encompassed a message, an expression of B. L.'s irritation with, and criticism of, the school and cheerleading communities. . . .

Second, the school argues that it was trying to prevent disruption [within] the bounds of a school-sponsored extracurricular activity. But we can find no evidence [of] the sort of "substantial disruption" of a school activity or a threatened harm to the rights of others that might justify the school's action. Rather, the record shows that discussion of the matter took, at most, 5 to 10 minutes of an Algebra class "for just a couple of days" and that some members of the cheerleading team were "upset" about the content of B. L.'s Snapchats. [As] we said in *Tinker*, "for the State in the person of school officials to justify prohibition of a particular expression of opinion, it must be able to show that its action was caused by something more than a mere desire to avoid the discomfort and unpleasantness that always accompany an unpopular viewpoint."

Third, the school presented some evidence that expresses [a] concern for team morale. There is [little,] however, that suggests any serious decline in team morale—to the point where it could create a substantial interference in, or disruption of, the school's efforts to maintain team cohesion. As we have said [in *Tinker*,] simple "undifferentiated fear or apprehension . . . is not enough to overcome the right to freedom of expression."

[Although] we do not agree with the reasoning of the Third Circuit majority, [we] agree that the school violated B. L.'s First Amendment rights. [Affirmed.]

JUSTICE ALITO, with whom JUSTICE GORSUCH joins, concurring.

I join the opinion of the Court but write separately to explain [the] framework within which I think cases like this should be analyzed. This is the first case in which we have considered [a] public school's attempt to regulate true off-premises student speech, and it is important that our opinion not be misunderstood.[2]

The Court holds—and I agree—that: the First Amendment permits public schools to regulate *some* student speech that does not occur on school premises during the regular school day. [I] also agree that it is not prudent for us to attempt at this time to "set forth a broad, highly general First Amendment rule" governing all off-premises speech. But [it] is helpful to consider the framework within which efforts to regulate off-premises speech should be analyzed.

---

[2] [Ct's Note] This case does not involve speech by a student at a public college or university. For several reasons, including the age, independence, and living arrangements of such students, regulation of their speech may raise very different questions from those presented here. I do not understand the decision in this case to apply to such students.

[I] start with this threshold question: Why does the First Amendment ever allow the free-speech rights of public school students to be restricted to a greater extent than the rights of other juveniles who do not attend a public school? As the Court recognized in *Tinker*, when a public school regulates student speech, it acts as an arm of the State in which it is located. Suppose that B. L. had been enrolled in a private school and did exactly what she did in this case. [Pennsylvania] would have had no legal basis to punish her and almost certainly would not have even tried. So why should her status as a public school student give the Commonwealth any greater authority to punish her speech?

Our cases involving the regulation of student speech have not directly addressed this question. All those cases involved either in-school speech or speech that was tantamount to in-school speech. And in those cases, the Court appeared to take it for granted that "the special characteristics of the school environment" justified special rules. Why the Court took this for granted is not hard to imagine. As a practical matter, it is impossible to see how a school could function if administrators and teachers could not regulate on-premises student speech, including by imposing content-based restrictions in the classroom. In a math class, for example, the teacher can insist that students talk about math, not some other subject. In addition, when a teacher asks a question, the teacher must have the authority to insist that the student respond to that question and not some other question, and a teacher must also have the authority to speak without interruption and to demand that students refrain from interrupting one another. Practical necessity likewise dictates that teachers and school administrators have related authority with respect to other in-school activities like auditorium programs attended by a large audience. [But] when a public school regulates what students say or write when they are not on school grounds and are not participating in a school program, the school has the obligation to answer the question with which I began: Why should enrollment in a public school result in the diminution of a student's free-speech rights? The only plausible answer [is that] by enrolling a child in a public school, parents consent on behalf of the child to the relinquishment of some of the child's free-speech rights.

[When] it comes to children, courts [have] analyzed the issue of consent by adapting the common-law doctrine of *in loco parentis*. Under the common law, as Blackstone explained, "[a father could] delegate part of his parental authority . . . to the tutor or schoolmaster of his child; who is then *in loco parentis*, and has *such a portion of the power of the parent* committed to his charge, [namely,] that of restraint and correction, *as may be necessary to answer the purposes for which he is employed*." [Today,] of course, the educational picture is quite different. [If] *in loco parentis* is transplanted [to] the 21st century United States, what it amounts to is simply a doctrine of inferred parental consent to a public school's exercise of a degree of authority that is commensurate with the task that the parents ask the school to perform. [So] how much authority to regulate speech do parents implicitly delegate when they enroll a child at a public school? The answer must be that parents are treated as having relinquished the measure of authority that the schools must be able to exercise in order to carry out their state-mandated educational mission, as well as the authority to perform any other functions to which parents expressly or implicitly agree—for example, by giving permission for a child to participate in an extracurricular activity or to go on a school trip.

I have already explained what this delegated authority means with respect to student speech during standard classroom instruction. And [this] authority extends to periods when students are in school but are not in class, for example, when they are walking in a hall, eating lunch, congregating outside before the school day starts, or waiting for a bus after school. [A] public school's regulation of off-premises student speech is a different matter. While the decision to enroll a student in a public school may be regarded as conferring the authority to regulate *some* off-premises speech, [enrollment] cannot be treated as a complete transfer of parental authority over a student's speech. [It] would be far-fetched to suggest that enrollment implicitly confers the right to regulate what a child says or writes at all times of day and throughout the calendar year.

[The] degree to which enrollment in a public school can be regarded as a delegation of authority over off-campus speech depends on the nature of the speech and the circumstances under which it occurs. [One] category of off-premises student speech falls easily within the scope of the authority that parents implicitly or explicitly provide. This category includes speech that takes place during or as part of what amounts to a temporal or spatial extension of the regular school program, *e.g.,* online instruction at home, assigned essays or other homework, and transportation to and from school. Also included are statements made during other school activities in which students participate with their parents' consent, such as school trips, school sports and other extracurricular activities that may take place after regular school hours or off school premises, and after-school programs for students who would otherwise be without adult supervision during that time. Abusive speech that occurs while students are walking to and from school may also fall into this category on the theory that it is school attendance that puts students on that route and in the company of the fellow students who engage in the abuse. The imperatives that justify the regulation of student speech while in school [apply] more or less equally to these off-premises activities.

[At] the other end of the spectrum, there is a category of speech that is almost always beyond the regulatory authority of a public school. This is student speech that is not expressly and specifically directed at the school, school administrators, teachers, or fellow students and that addresses matters of public concern, including sensitive subjects like politics, religion, and social relations. Speech on such matters lies at the heart of the First Amendment's protection, and the connection between student speech in this category and the ability of a public school to carry out its instructional program is tenuous. If a school tried to regulate such speech, the most that it could claim is that offensive off-premises speech on important matters may cause controversy and recriminations among students and may thus disrupt instruction and good order on school premises. But it is a "bedrock principle" that speech may not be suppressed simply because it expresses ideas that are "offensive or disagreeable."

[Between] these two extremes (*i.e.*, off-premises speech that is tantamount to on-campus speech and general statements made off premises on matters of public concern) lie the categories of off-premises student speech that appear to have given rise to the most litigation. A survey of lower court cases reveals several prominent categories. [One] group of cases involves perceived threats to school administrators, teachers, other staff members, or students. Laws that apply to everyone prohibit defined categories of threats. [Another] common category involves speech that criticizes or derides school administrators, teachers, or other staff members. Schools may assert that parents who send their children to a public school implicitly authorize the school to demand that the child exhibit the respect that is required for orderly and effective instruction, but parents surely do not relinquish their children's ability to complain in an appropriate manner about wrongdoing, dereliction, or even plain incompetence. Perhaps the most difficult category involves criticism or hurtful remarks about other students. Bullying and severe harassment are serious (and age-old) problems, but these concepts are not easy to define with the precision required for a regulation of speech.

The present case does not fall into any of these categories. Instead, it simply involves criticism (albeit in a crude manner) of the school and an extracurricular activity. Unflattering speech about a school or one of its programs is different from speech that criticizes or derides particular individuals, and [the] school's justifications for punishing B. L.'s speech were weak. [The] school did not claim that the messages caused any significant disruption of classes. [As] for the messages' effect on the morale of the cheerleading squad, the coach of a team sport may wish to take group cohesion and harmony into account in selecting members of the team, in assigning roles, and in allocating playing time, but it is self-evident that this authority has limits. [There] is, finally, the matter of B. L.'s language. There are parents who would not have been pleased with B. L.'s language and gesture, but whatever B. L.'s parents thought about what she did, it is not reasonable to infer that they gave the school the authority to regulate her choice of language when she was off school premises and not engaged in any school activity.

[The] overwhelming majority of school administrators, teachers, and coaches are men and women who are deeply dedicated to the best interests of their students, but it is predictable that there will be occasions when some will get carried away, as did the school officials in the case at hand. If today's decision teaches any lesson, it must be that the regulation of many types of off-premises student speech raises serious First Amendment concerns, and school officials should proceed cautiously before venturing into this territory.

JUSTICE THOMAS, dissenting.

B. L., a high school student, sent a profanity-laced message to hundreds of people, including classmates and team- mates. The message included a picture of B. L. raising her middle finger and captioned "F*** school" and "f*** cheer." This message was juxtaposed with another, which explained that B. L. was frustrated that she failed to make the varsity cheerleading squad. The cheerleading coach responded by disciplining B. L.

The Court overrides that decision—without even mentioning the 150 years of history supporting the coach. [When] students are on campus, the majority says, schools have authority *in loco parentis* [to] discipline speech and conduct. Off campus, the authority of schools is somewhat less. At that level of generality, I agree. But the majority omits important detail. What authority does a school have when it operates *in loco parentis*? How much less authority do schools have over off-campus speech and conduct? And how does a court decide if speech is on or off campus?

Disregarding these important issues, the majority simply posits three vague considerations and reaches an outcome. A more searching review reveals that schools historically could discipline students in circumstances like those presented here. Because the majority does not attempt to explain why we should not apply this historical rule and does not attempt to tether its approach to anything stable, I respectfully dissent.

[While] the majority entirely ignores the relevant history, I would begin the assessment of the scope of free-speech rights incorporated against the States by looking to "what 'ordinary citizens' at the time of [the Fourteenth Amendment's] ratification would have understood" the right to encompass. Cases and treatises from that era reveal that public schools retained substantial authority to discipline students: [A school could] regulate speech when it occurs off campus, so long as it has a proximate tendency to harm the school, its faculty or students, or its programs. [If] there is a good constitutional reason to depart from this historical rule, the majority and the parties fail to identify it.

[Our] modern doctrine is not to the contrary. "[T]he penalties imposed in this case were unrelated to any political viewpoint" or religious viewpoint. And although the majority sugar coats this speech as "criticism," it is well settled that schools can punish "vulgar" speech—at least when it occurs on campus. The discipline here—a 1-year suspension from the team—may strike some as disproportionate. But [there is] no textual or historical evidence to suggest that federal courts generally can police the proportionality of school disciplinary decisions in the name of the First Amendment.

The majority declines to consider [this] history, instead favoring a few pragmatic guideposts. [Consider] the Court's longtime failure to grapple with the historical doctrine of *in loco parentis*. [The] Fourteenth Amendment was ratified against the background legal principle that publicly funded schools operated [as] delegated substitutes of parents. This principle freed schools from the constraints the Fourteenth Amendment placed on other government actors. [Plausible] arguments can be raised in favor of departing from that historical doctrine. When the Fourteenth Amendment was ratified, just three jurisdictions had compulsory-education laws. One might argue that [*in*] *loco parentis* applies only when delegation is voluntary. The Court, however, did not make that (or any other) argument against this historical doctrine. [It] acknowledges that schools act *in loco parentis* when students speak on campus [but] fails to address the historical contours of that doctrine, whether the doctrine applies to off-campus speech, or why the Court has abandoned it. [Moreover,] the majority uncritically adopts the assumption that B. L.'s speech, in fact, was off campus. But the location of her speech is a much trickier question than the majority acknowledges. Because speech travels, schools sometimes may be able to treat speech as on campus even though it originates off campus. Nobody doubts, for example, that a school . . . can discipline [a student] when he passes out vulgar flyers on campus—even if he creates those flyers off campus. The same may be true in many contexts when social media speech is generated off campus but received on campus. [Here,] it makes sense to treat B. L.'s speech as off-campus speech. There is little evidence that B. L.'s speech was received on campus. [But] the majority mentions none of this. It simply, and uncritically, assumes that B. L.'s speech was off campus. . . .

[The] Court transparently takes a common-law approach to today's decision. It states just one rule: Schools can regulate speech less often when that speech occurs off campus. It then identifies this case as an "example" and "leav[es] for future cases" the job of developing this new common-law doctrine. But the Court's foundation is untethered from anything stable, and courts (and schools) will almost certainly be at a loss as to what exactly the Court's opinion today means. [Because] it reaches the wrong result under the appropriate historical test, I respectfully dissent.

III. GOVERNMENT AS EMPLOYER

P. 1102, add at end of Note 6:

For application and extensive discussion of the *Pickering-Garcetti* framework in the context of religious speech by a high school football coach, see *Kennedy v. Bremerton School District* (2022, Supp. to Ch. 8, Sec. 2 infra).

9. THE RIGHT NOT TO SPEAK, THE RIGHT TO ASSOCIATE, AND THE RIGHT NOT TO ASSOCIATE

I. THE RIGHT NOT TO BE ASSOCIATED WITH PARTICULAR IDEAS

P. 1149, add at end of footnote 285:

A Texas statute, HB20, prohibits non-governmental social media platforms with at least 50 million active users from "censor[ing]" users and uses based in viewpoint. Two social media trade associations challenged the statute, arguing that platforms had their own First Amendment rights to select and deselect based in content. The United States District Court for the Western District of Texas agreed, and preliminarily enjoined enforcement of the statute, but the Fifth Circuit stayed the preliminary injunction. An application to the Supreme Court to vacate the stay, and thus to continue to enjoin operation if HB20, was granted, *Netchoice, LLC v. Paxton*, 142 S.Ct 1715 (2022), with Justice Kagan noting without opinion that she would deny the application to vacate the stay, and thus continue the injunction against enforcement of HB20. Justice Alito, joined by Justices Thomas and Gorsuch, also dissented from the decision to vacate the stay, discussing at length the importance of the question of the susceptibility under the First Amendment of regulation of private social media platforms, and arguing that the Court should not yet interfere with the proceedings below.

P. 1162, add as new note 10 after note 9:

10. *Compelled disclosures revisited.* Both *NAACP v. Alabama, supra,* and *Shelton v. Tucker*, 364 U.S. 479 (1960), dealt with Civil Rights era attempts to intimidate civil rights organization by requiring disclosure of membership lists. In *Americans for Prosperity Foundation v. Bonta*, 141 S.Ct. 2373 (2021), the Court revisited that issue and seemed to extend and strengthen that aspect of the freedom of association, even outside of the civil rights context and even absent evidence of the kind of actual or potential intimidation that was at issue in *NAACP* and *Shelton*.

At issue in *Americans for Prosperity* was a challenge to a California Attorney General's regulation, adopted and administered pursuant to the Attorney General's statutory authority to regulate charitable organizations, requiring that regulated charities disclose their major donors, typically those whose donations were $5000 per year or more. Two charitable organizations, one (Americans for Prosperity) with a focus on economic liberty and related issues, and the other (Thomas More Law Center) focused substantially on issues of religious freedom, challenged the donor disclosure requirement, and the Court, per ROBERTS, C.J., upheld the challenge, relying on *NAACP* and *Shelton* and finding the restriction to be an unjustified restriction on the First Amendment's implicit protection of freedom of expression.

Four issues dominated the various opinions. One was the level of scrutiny. Neither *NAACP* nor *Shelton* had specified the appropriate level of scrutiny for compelled membership or donor disclosures, but the Court in *Buckley v. Valeo* (1976, sec. 10, *infra*) had held that required disclosures in the campaign finance context must be measured under a standard of "exacting scrutiny." And although one of the challenging organizations had argued that exacting scrutiny was the equivalent of strict scrutiny, with the latter's requirement of "the least restrictive alternative," the Court in *Americans for Prosperity* held that exacting scrutiny was as applicable outside of the campaign and election context as within it, and that it required both a "sufficiently important governmental interest" and means of pursuing that interest that were "narrowly tailored," although not the least restrictive alternative. "Where exacting scrutiny applies, the challenged requirement must be narrowly tailored to the interest it promotes, even if it is not the least restrictive means of achieving that end."

Reversing the Ninth Circuit, the Court found California's interest in "preventing wrongdoing by charitable organizations" sufficiently important, but concluded that the disclosure requirement was not narrowly tailored to achieve that end. "In reality, then, California's interest is less in investigating fraud and more in ease of administration. . . . But [mere] administrative convenience does not remotely 'reflect the seriousness of the actual burden.' *Doe v. Reed*, 561 U.S. 186 (2010)."

The second issue was the existence or not of an actual threat of actual donor intimidation. Finding the possibility of actual intimidation remote and speculative, SOTOMAYOR, J., joined by Breyer and Kagan, JJ, dissenting, insisted that this case differed substantially from both *NAACP* and *Shelton*, where there had been actual evidence of genuinely threatened intimidation: "[Not] all reporting and disclosure regimes burden associational rights in the same way. [Regardless] of whether there is any risk of public disclosure, and no matter if the burdens on associational rights are slight, heavy, or non-existent, disclosure regimes must [now] be narrowly tailored. The Court searches in vain to find a foothold for this new approach. . . . [Today's] decision discards decades of First Amendment jurisprudence recognizing that reporting and disclosure requirements do not directly burden associational rights."

The third issue was whether the alleged defects in California's approach justified a facial challenge and thus facial invalidation. Under the majority's approach, which it labeled an application of First Amendment overbreadth doctrine, "the lack of tailoring to the State's investigative goal is categorical—present in every case—as is the weakness of the State's interest in administrative convenience. Every demand that might chill association therefore fails exacting scrutiny." And although Justice Sotomayor's dissent implied that she might not even have found intimidation or chilling with respect to these particular challengers, she argued more strongly that the case was inappropriate for facial invalidation: "If the Court had simply granted as-applied relief to petitioners based on its reading of the facts [and the fear of reprisals by these donors], I would be sympathetic, although my own views diverge. [But] the Court jettisons completely the longstanding requirement that plaintiffs demonstrate an actual burden [to them] before the Court will subject governmental action to close scrutiny. It then invalidates a regulation in its entirety, even though it can point to no record evidence demonstrating that the regulation is likely to chill a substantial proportion of donors."[1]

[1]   Thomas, J., joining the majority in all except its decision to characterize the case as a facial challenge, objected once again to the Court's overbreadth doctrine, and objected to characterizing it as either an overbreadth claim or a facial challenge: "The Court simply (and correctly) holds that the District Court properly enjoined the law *as applied* to petitioners." "A declaration that the law is 'facially' unconstitutional' seems to me no more than an advisory opinion—which a federal court should never issue at all." Alito, J., joined by Gorsuch, J., also joined all of the majority opinion except for its discussion of the distinction between exacting and strict scrutiny, seeing "no need to decide [now] which standard should be applied here or whether the same level of scrutiny should apply in all [compelled disclosure] cases."

10. WEALTH, EQUALITY, AND THE POLITICAL PROCESS

P. 1179, add as new paragraph at end of footnote 305:

Do disclosure requirements, even without limitations on the amounts, create First Amendment problems in campaign finance context? The issue lurked in the vicinity of *Americans for Prosperity Foundation v. Bonta*, 141 S.Ct. 2373 (2021), discussed above, addition to p. 1162.

P. 1193, add as new note 10:

10. *Use of contributions.* FEC v. CRUZ, 142 S.Ct. 1638 (2022), dealt with the issue of personal loans by candidates for federal office to their campaign committees. Under the complex rules of the Bipartisan Campaign Reform Act of 2002, candidates are permitted to loan their own money to their campaign committees, and those committees are allowed to repay the loans from contributions from other donors. But because of the perceived risk of corruption, post-election contributions may be used to repay candidate personal loans only up to $250,000 except for a 20-day post-election window. Senator Ted Cruz of Texas challenged the $250,000 limitation as a violation of the First Amendment right of candidates to use their own money to support the cause of their own candidacy, and the Supreme Court agreed, with ROBERTS, C.J., writing for the 6–3 majority.

The majority perceived the repayment limitation as "increasing the risk" that candidates loaning their own money to their campaigns will not be repaid, a possibility that "inhibits candidates from loaning money to their campaigns in the first place, burdening core speech." Because "the ability to lend money to a campaign is especially important for new candidates and challengers," the majority reasoned, restrictions or inhibitions in the name of preventing the appearance or actuality of quid pro quo corruption would have to be justified by evidence of the actual or likely existence of such corruption, evidence the majority claimed was completely absent. Moreover, the majority argued, deference to congressional judgment "would be especially inappropriate" where a legislative act has the potential of insulating the enacting legislators from effective challenges to their own positions.

KAGAN, J., dissented, joined by Breyer and Sotomayor, JJ. She argued that successful candidates wishing to recoup their own expenditures would have good reason to solicit post-election contributions, and donors wishing favorable legislative treatment for their own projects and interests would have good reason to contribute to winning candidates. This combination of incentives made corruption especially likely, she argued, a likelihood that was sufficient to justify the restriction. "In striking down the law today, the Court greenlights all the sordid bargains Congress thought right to stop." Moreover, the candidate even in the face of the restriction "can in fact *self*-fund all he likes. The law impedes only his ability use *other people's money* to finance his campaign—much as standard (and permissible) contribution limits do."

CHAPTER 8

FREEDOM OF RELIGION

▪ ▪ ▪

1. THE ESTABLISHMENT CLAUSE

II. AID TO RELIGION

P. 1218, replacing Zelman v. Simmons-Harris, *or* P. 1230, after Zelman v. Simmons-Harris, *or* P. 1305, after Espinoza (Supplement):

CARSON V. MAKIN

___ U.S. ___, 142 S.Ct. 1987, ___ L.Ed.2d ___ (2022).

CHIEF JUSTICE ROBERTS delivered the opinion of the Court.

Maine has enacted a program of tuition assistance for parents who live in school districts that do not operate a secondary school of their own. Under the program, parents designate the secondary school they would like their child to attend—public or private—and the school district transmits payments to that school to help defray the costs of tuition. Most private schools are eligible to receive the payments, so long as they are "nonsectarian." The question presented is whether this restriction violates the Free Exercise Clause of the First Amendment.

I

A

Maine's Constitution provides that the State's legislature shall "require . . . the several towns to make suitable provision, at their own expense, for the support and maintenance of public schools." In accordance with that command, the legislature has required that every school-age child in Maine "shall be provided an opportunity to receive the benefits of a free public education," and that the required schools be operated by "the legislative and governing bodies of local school administrative units," But Maine is the most rural State in the Union, and for many school districts the realities of remote geography and low population density make those commands difficult to heed. Indeed, of Maine's 260 school administrative units (SAUs), fewer than half operate a public secondary school of their own.

Maine has sought to deal with this problem in part by creating a program of tuition assistance for families that reside in such areas. Under that program, if an SAU neither operates its own public secondary school nor contracts with a particular public or private school for the education of its school-age children, the SAU must "pay the tuition . . . at the public school or the approved private school of the parent's choice at which the student is accepted." Parents who wish to take advantage of this benefit first select the school they wish their child to attend. If they select a private school that has been "approved" by the Maine Department of Education, the parents' SAU "shall pay the tuition" at the chosen school up to a specified maximum rate.

To be "approved" to receive these payments, a private school must meet certain basic requirements under Maine's compulsory education law. [But the] program imposes no geographic limitation: Parents may direct tuition payments to schools inside or outside the State, or even in foreign countries. [Prior] to 1981, parents could also direct the tuition assistance payments to religious schools. [In] 1981, however, Maine imposed a new requirement that any school receiving tuition assistance payments must be "a nonsectarian school in accordance with the First Amendment of the United States Constitution." That provision was enacted in response to an opinion by the Maine attorney general taking the position that public funding of private religious schools violated the Establishment Clause of the First Amendment. We subsequently held, however, that a benefit program under which private citizens "direct government aid to religious schools wholly as a result of their own genuine and independent private choice" does not offend the Establishment Clause. *Zelman* v. *Simmons-Harris* (2002, Sec. 1, I supra) Following our decision in *Zelman*, the Maine Legislature considered a proposed bill to repeal the "nonsectarian" requirement, but rejected it.

The "nonsectarian" requirement for participation in Maine's tuition assistance program remains in effect today. The Department has stated that, in administering this requirement, it "considers a sectarian school to be one that is associated with a particular faith or belief system and which, in addition to teaching academic subjects, promotes the faith or belief system with which it is associated and/or presents the material taught through the lens of this faith." "The Department's focus is on what the school teaches through its curriculum and related activities, and how the material is presented." "[A]ffiliation or association with a church or religious institution is one potential indicator of a sectarian school," but "it is not dispositive."

B

This case concerns two families that live in SAUs that neither maintain their own secondary schools nor contract with any nearby secondary school. Petitioners David and Amy Carson reside in Glenburn, Maine. When this litigation commenced, the Carsons' daughter attended high school at Bangor Christian Schools (BCS), which was founded in 1970 as a ministry of Bangor Baptist Church. [Petitioners] Troy and Angela Nelson live in Palermo, Maine. When this litigation commenced, the Nelsons' [son] attended middle school at Temple Academy, a "sectarian" school affiliated with Centerpoint Community Church. The Nelsons sent their son to Temple Academy because they believed it offered him a high-quality education that aligned with their sincerely held religious beliefs. . . .

[In] 2018, petitioners brought suit against the commissioner of the Maine Department of Education. They alleged that the "nonsectarian" requirement of Maine's tuition assistance program violated the Free Exercise Clause and the Establishment Clause of the First Amendment. [While] petitioners' appeal to the First Circuit was pending, this Court decided *Espinoza* v. *Montana Department of Revenue* (2020, Supp. to p. 1305 infra). [The] First Circuit recognized that, in light of *Espinoza*, its prior precedent upholding Maine's "nonsectarian" requirement was no longer controlling. But it nevertheless affirmed the District Court's grant of judgment to the commissioner.

As relevant here, the First Circuit offered two grounds to distinguish Maine's "nonsectarian" requirement from the no-aid provision at issue in *Espinoza*. First, the panel reasoned that, whereas Montana had barred schools from receiving funding "simply based on their religious identity—a status that in and of itself does not determine how a school would use the funds"—Maine bars BCS and Temple Academy from receiving funding "based on the religious use that they would make of it in instructing children." Second, the panel determined that Maine's tuition assistance program was distinct from the scholarships at issue in *Espinoza* because Maine had sought to provide "a rough equivalent of the public school education that Maine may permissibly require to be secular but that is not otherwise accessible." Thus, "the nature of the restriction at issue and the nature of the school aid program of which it is a key part" led the panel to conclude "once again" that Maine's "nonsectarian" requirement did not violate the Free Exercise Clause.

II

A

[We] have repeatedly held that a State violates the Free Exercise Clause when it excludes religious observers from otherwise available public benefits. [Two] Terms ago, in *Espinoza*, we reached the same conclusion as to a Montana program that provided tax credits to donors who sponsored scholarships for private school tuition. . . .

B

The "unremarkable" principles applied in [*Espinoza*] suffice to resolve this case. Maine offers its citizens a benefit: tuition assistance payments for any family whose school district does not provide a public secondary school. Just like the wide range of nonprofit organizations eligible to receive playground resurfacing grants in *Trinity Lutheran Church of Columbus v. Comer* (2017, Sec. 2, I infra), a wide range of private schools are eligible to receive Maine tuition assistance payments here. And like the daycare center in *Trinity Lutheran*, BCS and Temple Academy are disqualified from this generally available benefit "solely because of their religious character." . . .

Our recent decision in *Espinoza* applied these basic principles in the context of religious education that we consider today. There, as here, we considered a state benefit program under which public funds flowed to support tuition payments at private schools. And there, as here, that program specifically carved out private religious schools from those eligible to receive such funds. While the wording of the Montana and Maine provisions is different, their effect is the same: to "disqualify some private schools" from funding "solely because they are religious." A law that operates in that manner [must] be subjected to "the strictest scrutiny."

To satisfy strict scrutiny, government action "must advance 'interests of the highest order' and must be narrowly tailored in pursuit of those interests." "A law that targets religious conduct for distinctive treatment . . . will survive strict scrutiny only in rare cases." This is not one of them. As noted, a neutral benefit program in which public funds flow to religious organizations through the independent choices of private benefit recipients does not offend the Establishment Clause. *Zelman.* But as we explained in both *Trinity Lutheran* and *Espinoza*, [an] "interest in separating church and state 'more fiercely' than the Federal Constitution . . . 'cannot qualify as compelling' in the face of the infringement of free exercise." . . .

III

The First Circuit attempted to distinguish our precedent by recharacterizing the nature of Maine's tuition assistance program in two ways, both of which Maine echoes before this Court. First, the panel defined the benefit at issue as the "rough equivalent of [a Maine] public school education," an education that cannot include sectarian instruction. Second, the panel defined the nature of the exclusion as one based not on a school's religious "status," as in *Trinity Lutheran* and *Espinoza*, but on religious "uses" of public funds. Neither of these formal distinctions suffices to distinguish this case from *Trinity Lutheran* or *Espinoza*, or to affect the application of the free exercise principles outlined above.

A

The First Circuit held that the "nonsectarian" requirement was constitutional because the benefit was properly viewed not as tuition assistance payments to be used at approved private schools, but instead as funding for the "rough equivalent of the public school education that Maine may permissibly require to be secular."

To start with, the statute does not say anything like that. It says that an SAU without a secondary school of its own "shall pay the tuition . . . at the public school or the approved private school of the parent's choice at which the student is accepted." The benefit is *tuition* at a public *or* private school, selected by the parent, with no suggestion that the "private school" must somehow provide a "public" education. . . .

Moreover, the curriculum taught at participating private schools need not even resemble that taught in the Maine public schools. For example, Maine public schools must abide by certain "parameters for essential instruction in English language arts; mathematics; science and technology; social studies; career and education development; visual and performing arts; health, physical education and wellness; and world languages." But accredited private schools are exempt from these requirements, and instead subject only to general "standards and indicators" governing the implementation of their own chosen curriculum. There are other distinctions, too. Participating schools need not hire state-certified teachers. And the schools can be single-sex. In short, it is simply not the case that these schools, to be eligible for state funds, must offer an education that is equivalent—roughly or otherwise—to that available in the Maine public schools.

But the key manner in which the two educational experiences *are* required to be "equivalent" is that they must both be secular. Saying that Maine offers a benefit limited to private secular education is just another way of saying that Maine does not extend tuition assistance payments to parents who choose to educate their children at religious schools. [Indeed,] were we to accept Maine's argument, our decision in *Espinoza* would be rendered essentially meaningless. By Maine's logic, Montana could have obtained the same result that we held violated the First Amendment simply by redefining its tax credit for sponsors of generally available scholarships as limited to "tuition payments for the rough equivalent of a Montana public education"—meaning a secular education. But our holding in *Espinoza* turned on the substance of free exercise protections, not on the presence or absence of magic words. That holding applies fully whether the prohibited discrimination is in an express provision like § 2951(2) or in a party's reconceptualization of the public benefit.

Maine may provide a strictly secular education in its public schools. But BCS and Temple Academy—like numerous other recipients of Maine tuition assistance payments—are not public schools. In order to provide an education to children who live in certain parts of its far-flung State, Maine has decided *not* to operate schools of its own, but instead to offer tuition assistance that parents may direct to the public or private schools of *their* choice. Maine's administration of that benefit is subject to the free exercise principles governing any such public benefit program—including the prohibition on denying the benefit based on a recipient's religious exercise. . . . [As] we held in *Espinoza*, a "State need not subsidize private education. But once a State decides to do so, it cannot disqualify some private schools solely because they are religious."

B

The Court of Appeals also attempted to distinguish this case from *Trinity Lutheran* and *Espinoza* on the ground that the funding restrictions in those cases were "solely status-based religious discrimination," while the challenged provision here "imposes a use-based restriction." Justice Breyer makes the same argument. [That argument,], however, misreads our precedents. In *Trinity Lutheran* and *Espinoza*, we held that the Free Exercise Clause forbids discrimination on the basis of religious status. But those decisions never suggested that use-based discrimination is any less offensive to the Free Exercise Clause. [Any] attempt to give effect to such a distinction by scrutinizing whether and how a religious school pursues its educational mission would also raise serious concerns about state entanglement with religion and denominational favoritism. [In] short, the prohibition on status-based discrimination under the Free Exercise Clause is not a permission to engage in use-based discrimination. . . .

[Maine's] "nonsectarian" requirement for its otherwise generally available tuition assistance payments violates the Free Exercise Clause of the First Amendment. Regardless of how the benefit and restriction are described, the program operates to identify and exclude otherwise eligible schools on the basis of their religious exercise.

[Reversed].

JUSTICE BREYER, with whom JUSTICE KAGAN joins, and with whom JUSTICE SOTOMAYOR joins except as to Part I-B, dissenting.

The First Amendment begins by forbidding the government from "mak[ing] [any] law respecting an establishment of religion." It next forbids them to make any law "prohibiting the free exercise thereof." The Court today pays almost no attention to the words in the first Clause while giving almost exclusive attention to the words in the second. The majority also fails to recognize the " 'play in the joints' " between the two Clauses. See *Trinity Lutheran Church*. That "play" gives States some degree of legislative leeway. It sometimes allows a State to further antiestablishment interests by withholding aid from religious institutions without violating the Constitution's protections for the free exercise of religion. In my view, Maine's nonsectarian requirement falls squarely within the scope of that constitutional leeway. I respectfully dissent.

I

A

The First Amendment's two Religion Clauses together provide that the government "shall make no law respecting an establishment of religion, or prohibiting the free exercise thereof." Each Clause, linguistically speaking, is "cast in absolute terms." The Establishment Clause seems to bar all government "sponsorship, financial support, [or] active involvement . . . in religious activity," while the Free Exercise Clause seems to bar all "governmental restraint on religious practice." The apparently absolutist nature of these two prohibitions means that either Clause, "if expanded to a logical extreme, would tend to clash with the other." Because of this, we have said, the two Clauses "are frequently in tension," and "often exert conflicting pressures" on government action.

[Although] the Religion Clauses are, in practice, often in tension, they nonetheless "express complementary values." Together they attempt to chart a "course of constitutional neutrality" with respect to government and religion. They were written to help create an American Nation free of the religious conflict that had long plagued European nations with "governmentally established religion[s]." Through the Clauses, the Framers sought to avoid the "anguish, hardship and bitter strife" that resulted from the "union of Church and State" in those countries.

The Religion Clauses thus created a compromise in the form of religious freedom. [And] in applying these Clauses, we have often said that "there is room for play in the joints" between them. This doctrine reflects the fact that it may be difficult to determine in any particular case whether the Free Exercise Clause *requires* a State to fund the activities of a religious institution, or whether the Establishment Clause *prohibits* the State from doing so. Rather than attempting to draw a highly reticulated and complex free-exercise/establishment line that varies based on the specific circumstances of each state-funded program, we have provided general interpretive principles that apply uniformly in all Religion Clause cases. At the same time, we have made clear that States enjoy a degree of freedom to navigate the Clauses' competing prohibitions. This includes choosing not to fund certain religious activity where States have strong, establishment-related reasons for not doing so. And, States have freedom to make this choice even when the Establishment Clause does not itself prohibit the State from funding that activity. The Court today nowhere mentions, and I fear effectively abandons, this longstanding doctrine.

B

I have previously discussed my views of the relationship between the Religion Clauses and how I believe these Clauses should be interpreted to advance their goal of avoiding religious strife. [This] potential for religious strife is still with us. We are today a Nation with well over 100 different religious groups, from Free Will Baptist to African Methodist, Buddhist to Humanist. People in our country adhere to a vast array of beliefs, ideals, and philosophies. And with greater religious diversity comes greater risk of religiously based strife, conflict, and social division. The Religion Clauses were written in part to help avoid that disunion. As Thomas Jefferson, one of the leading drafters and proponents of those Clauses, wrote, " 'to compel a man to furnish contributions of money for the propagation of opinions which he disbelieves, is sinful and tyrannical.' " And as James Madison, another drafter and proponent, said, compelled taxpayer sponsorship of religion "is itself a signal of persecution." . . .

I have also previously explained why I believe that a "rigid, bright-line" approach to the Religion Clauses—an approach without any leeway or "play in the joints"—will too often work against the Clauses' underlying purposes. [In] a word, to interpret the two Clauses as if they were joined at the hip will work against their basic purpose: to allow for an American society with practitioners of over 100 different religions, and those who do not practice religion at all, to live together without serious risk of religion-based social divisions.

II

The majority believes that the principles set forth in this Court's earlier cases easily resolve this case. But they do not.

We have previously found, as the majority points out, that "a neutral benefit program in which public funds flow to religious organizations through the independent choices of private benefit recipients does not offend the Establishment Clause." We have thus concluded that a State *may*, consistent with the Establishment Clause, provide funding to religious schools through a general public funding program if the "government aid . . . reach[es] religious institutions only by way of the deliberate choices of . . . individual [aid] recipients." But the key word is "may." We have never previously held what the Court holds today, namely, that a State *must* (not *may*) use state funds to pay for religious education as part of a tuition program designed to ensure the provision of free statewide public school education.

What happens once "may" becomes "must"? Does that transformation mean that a school district that pays for public schools must pay equivalent funds to parents who wish to send their children to religious schools? Does it mean that school districts that give vouchers for use at charter schools must pay equivalent funds to parents who wish to give their children a religious education? What other social benefits are there the State's provision of which means—under the majority's interpretation of the Free Exercise Clause—that the State must pay parents for the religious equivalent of the secular benefit provided? The concept of "play in the joints" means that courts need not, and should not, answer with "must" these questions that can more appropriately be answered with "may." . . .

III

A

I turn now to consider the Maine program at issue here. Maine's Constitution guarantees Maine's children a free public education by requiring that all towns provide "for the support and maintenance of public schools." [To] fulfill its constitutional promise, Maine created a program that provides some parents in these districts with a monetary grant to help them educate their children "at the public school or the approved private school of the parent's choice." . . .

Under Maine law, an "approved" private school must be "nonsectarian." A school fails to meet that requirement (and is deemed "sectarian") only if it is *both* (1) " 'associated with a particular faith or belief system' " *and also* (2) " 'promotes the faith or belief system with which it is associated and/or presents the [academic] material taught through the lens of this faith." To determine whether a school is sectarian, the " 'focus is on what the school teaches through its curriculum and related activities, and how the material is presented.' " " '[A]ffiliation or association with a church or religious institution . . . is not dispositive' " of sectarian status.

The two private religious schools at issue here satisfy both of these criteria. They are affiliated with a church or religious organization. And they also teach students to accept particular religious beliefs and to engage in particular religious practices.

The first school, Bangor Christian, has "educational objectives" that include " 'lead[ing] each unsaved student to trust Christ as his/her personal savior and then to follow Christ as Lord of his/her life,' " and " 'develop[ing] within each student a Christian world view and Christian philosophy of life.' " Bangor Christian "does not believe there is any way to separate the religious instruction from the academic instruction." Academic instruction and religious instruction are thus "completely intertwined." Bangor Christian teaches in its social studies class, for example, " 'that God has ordained evangelism.' " And in science class, students learn that atmospheric layers " 'are evidence of God's good design.' "

The second school, Temple Academy, similarly promotes religion through academics. Its "educational philosophy 'is based on a thoroughly Christian and Biblical world view.' " The school's "objectives" include " 'foster[ing] within each student an attitude of love and reverence of the

Bible as the infallible, inerrant, and authoritative Word of God.' " And the school's " 'academic growth' objectives" include " 'provid[ing] a sound academic education in which the subjec[t] areas are taught from a Christian point of view,' " and " 'help[ing] every student develop a truly Christian world view by integrating studies with the truths of Scripture.' " Like Bangor Christian, Temple "provides a 'biblically-integrated education,' which means that the Bible is used in every subject that is taught." In mathematics classes, for example, students learn that "a creator designed the universe such that 'one plus one is always going to be two.' "

The differences between this kind of education and a purely civic, public education are important. "The religious education and formation of students is the very reason for the existence of most private religious schools." [By] contrast, public schools, including those in Maine, seek first and foremost to provide a primarily civic education. [To] play that role effectively, public schools are religiously neutral, neither disparaging nor promoting any one particular system of religious beliefs. We accordingly have, as explained above, consistently required public school education to be free from religious affiliation or indoctrination.

Maine legislators who endorsed the State's nonsectarian requirement recognized these differences between public and religious education. They did not want Maine taxpayers to finance, through a tuition program designed to ensure the provision of free public education, schools that would use state money for teaching religious practices. See, *e.g.*, App. 104 (Maine representative stating that "[f]rom a public policy position, we must believe that a religiously neutral classroom is the best if funded by public dollars"); *id.*, at 106 (Maine senator asserting that the State's "limited [tax] dollars for schools" should be spent on those "that are non-religious and that are neutral on religion"). Underlying these views is the belief that the Establishment Clause seeks government neutrality. And the legislators thought that government payment for this kind of religious education would be antithetical to the religiously neutral education that the Establishment Clause requires in public schools. Maine's nonsectarian requirement, they believed, furthered the State's antiestablishment interests in not promoting religion in its public school system; the requirement prevented public funds—funds allocated to ensure that all children receive their constitutional right to a free public education—from being given to schools that would use the funds to promote religion.

In the majority's view, the fact that private individuals, not Maine itself, choose to spend the State's money on religious education saves Maine's program from Establishment Clause condemnation. But that fact, as I have said, simply *permits* Maine to route funds to religious schools. It does not *require* Maine to spend its money in that way. That is because, as explained above, this Court has long followed a legal doctrine that gives

States flexibility to navigate the tension between the two Religion Clauses. . . .

The Free Exercise Clause thus does not require Maine to fund, through its tuition program, schools that will use public money to promote religion. And considering the Establishment Clause concerns underlying the program, Maine's decision not to fund such schools falls squarely within the play in the joints between those two Clauses. Maine has promised all children within the State the right to receive a free public education. In fulfilling this promise, Maine endeavors to provide children the religiously neutral education required in public school systems. And that, in significant part, reflects the State's antiestablishment interests in avoiding spending public money to support what is essentially religious activity. The Religion Clauses give Maine the ability, and flexibility, to make this choice.

B

In my view, Maine's nonsectarian requirement is also constitutional because it supports, rather than undermines, the Religion Clauses' goal of avoiding religious strife. Forcing Maine to fund schools that provide the sort of religiously integrated education offered by Bangor Christian and Temple Academy creates a similar potential for religious strife as that raised by promoting religion in public schools. It may appear to some that the State favors a particular religion over others, or favors religion over nonreligion. Members of minority religions, with too few adherents to establish schools, may see injustice in the fact that only those belonging to more popular religions can use state money for religious education. Taxpayers may be upset at having to finance the propagation of religious beliefs that they do not share and with which they disagree. And parents in school districts that have a public secondary school may feel indignant that only *some* families in the State—those families in the more rural districts withoutpublic schools—have the opportunity to give their children a Maine-funded religious education.

[Maine's] nonsectarian requirement also serves to avoid religious strife between the State and the religious schools. Given that Maine is funding the schools as part of its effort to ensure that all children receive the basic public education to which they are entitled, Maine has an interest in ensuring that the education provided at these schools meets certain curriculum standards. Religious schools, on the other hand, have an interest in teaching a curriculum that advances the tenets of their religion. And the schools are of course entitled to teach subjects in the way that best reflects their religious beliefs. But the State may disagree with the particular manner in which the schools have decided that these subjects should be taught.

This is a situation ripe for conflict, as it forces Maine into the position of evaluating the adequacy or appropriateness of the schools' religiously inspired curriculum. Maine does not want this role. As one legislator explained, one of the reasons for the nonsectarian requirement was that "[g]overnment officials cannot, and should not, review the religious teachings of religious schools." Nor do the schools want Maine in this role. Bangor Christian asserted that it would only consider accepting public funds if it "did not have to make any changes in how it operates." Temple Academy similarly stated that it would only accept state money if it had "in writing that the school would not have to alter its admissions standards, hiring standards, or curriculum." The nonsectarian requirement ensures that Maine is not pitted against private religious schools in these battles over curriculum or operations, thereby avoiding the social strife resulting from this state-versus-religion confrontation. By invalidating the nonsectarian requirement, the majority today subjects the State, the schools, and the people of Maine to social conflict of a kind that they, and the Religion Clauses, sought to prevent. . . .

[Maine] wishes to provide children within the State with a secular, public education. This wish embodies, in significant part, the constitutional need to avoid spending public money to support what is essentially the teaching and practice of religion. That need is reinforced by the fact that we are today a Nation of more than 330 million people who ascribe to over 100 different religions. In that context, state neutrality with respect to religion is particularly important. The Religion Clauses give Maine the right to honor that neutrality by choosing not to fund religious schools as part of its public school tuition program. I believe the majority is wrong to hold the contrary. And with respect, I dissent.

JUSTICE SOTOMAYOR, dissenting.

This Court continues to dismantle the wall of separation between church and state that the Framers fought to build. Justice Breyer explains why the Court's analysis falters on its own terms, and I join all but Part I-B of his dissent. I write separately to add three points.

First, this Court should not have started down this path five years ago. Before *Trinity Lutheran*, it was well established that "both the United States and state constitutions embody distinct views" on "the subject of religion"—"in favor of free exercise, but opposed to establishment"—"that find no counterpart" with respect to other constitutional rights. Because of this tension, the Court recognized " 'room for play in the joints' between" the Religion Clauses, with "some state actions permitted by the Establishment Clause but not required by the Free Exercise Clause." Using this flexibility, and consistent with a rich historical tradition, States and the Federal Government could decline to fund religious institutions. Moreover, the Court for many decades understood the Establishment Clause to prohibit government from funding religious exercise.

Over time, the Court eroded these principles in certain respects. Nevertheless, the space between the Clauses continued to afford governments "some room to recognize the unique status of religious entities and to single them out on that basis for exclusion from otherwise generally applicable laws." *Trinity Lutheran* veered sharply away from that understanding. After assuming away an Establishment Clause violation, the Court revolutionized Free Exercise doctrine by equating a State's decision not to fund a religious organization with presumptively unconstitutional discrimination on the basis of religious status. A plurality, however, limited the Court's decision to "express discrimination based on religious identity" (*i.e.*, status), not "religious uses of funding." In other words, a State was barred from withholding funding from a religious entity "solely because of its religious character," but retained authority to do so on the basis that the funding would be put to religious uses. Two Terms ago, the Court reprised and extended *Trinity Lutheran*'s error to hold that a State could not limit a private-school voucher program to secular schools. Espinoza. The Court, however, again refrained from extending *Trinity Lutheran* from funding restrictions based on religious status to those based on religious uses.

As Justice Breyer explains, this status-use distinction readily distinguishes this case from *Trinity Lutheran* and *Espinoza*. I warned in *Trinity Lutheran*, however, that the Court's analysis could "be manipulated to call for a similar fate for lines drawn on the basis of religious use." That fear has come to fruition: The Court now holds for the first time that "any status-use distinction" is immaterial in both "theory" and "practice." It reaches that conclusion by embracing arguments from prior separate writings and ignoring decades of precedent affording governments flexibility in navigating the tension between the Religion Clauses. As a result, in just a few years, the Court has upended constitutional doctrine, shifting from a rule that permits States to decline to fund religious organizations to one that requires States in many circumstances to subsidize religious indoctrination with taxpayer dollars. . . .

[What] a difference five years makes. In 2017, I feared that the Court was "lead[ing] us . . . to a place where separation of church and state is a constitutional slogan, not a constitutional commitment." Today, the Court leads us to a place where separation of church and state becomes a constitutional violation. If a State cannot offer subsidies to its citizens without being required to fund religious exercise, any State that values its historic antiestablishment interests more than this Court does will have to curtail the support it offers to its citizens. With growing concern for where this Court will lead us next, I respectfully dissent.

III.   RELIGION AND PUBLIC SCHOOLS

P. 1249, after note 6:

KENNEDY V. BREMERTON SCHOOL DISTRICT
___ U.S. ___, 142 S.Ct. 2407, ___ L.Ed.2d ___ (2022).

JUSTICE GORSUCH delivered the opinion of the Court.

Joseph Kennedy lost his job as a high school football coach because he knelt at midfield after games to offer a quiet prayer of thanks. Mr. Kennedy prayed during a period when school employees were free to speak with a friend, call for a reservation at a restaurant, check email, or attend to other personal matters. He offered his prayers quietly while his students were otherwise occupied. Still, the Bremerton School District disciplined him anyway. It did so because it thought anything less could lead a reasonable observer to conclude (mistakenly) that it endorsed Mr. Kennedy's religious beliefs. That reasoning was misguided. . . .

I

A

Joseph Kennedy began working as a football coach at Bremerton High School in 2008 after nearly two decades of service in the Marine Corps. Like many other football players and coaches across the country, Mr. Kennedy made it a practice to give "thanks through prayer on the playing field" at the conclusion of each game. In his prayers, Kennedy sought to express gratitude for "what the players had accomplished and for the opportunity to be part of their lives through the game of football." Kennedy offered his prayers after the players and coaches had shaken hands, by taking a knee at the 50-yard line and praying "quiet[ly]" for "approximately 30 seconds."

Initially, Kennedy prayed on his own. But over time, some players asked whether they could pray alongside him. Kennedy responded by saying, " 'This is a free country. You can do what you want.' " The number of players who joined Kennedy eventually grew to include most of the team, at least after some games. Sometimes team members invited opposing players to join. Other times Kennedy still prayed alone. Eventually, he began incorporating short motivational speeches with his prayer when others were present. Separately, the team at times engaged in pregame or postgame prayers in the locker room. It seems this practice was a "school tradition" that predated Kennedy's tenure. Kennedy explained that he "never told any student that it was important they participate in any religious activity." In particular, he "never pressured or encouraged any student to join" his postgame midfield prayers.

For over seven years, no one complained to the Bremerton School District (District) about these practices. It seems the District's superintendent first learned of them only in September 2015, after an employee from another school commented positively on the school's practices to Bremerton's principal. At that point, the District reacted quickly. On September 17, the superintendent sent Mr. Kennedy a letter. In it, the superintendent identified "two problematic practices" in which Kennedy had engaged. First, he had provided "inspirational talk[s]" that included "overtly religious references" likely constituting "prayer" with the students "at midfield following the completion of . . . game[s]." Second, he had led "students and coaching staff in a prayer" in the locker-room tradition that "predated [his] involvement with the program."

The District explained that it sought to establish "clear parameters" "going forward." It instructed Kennedy to avoid any motivational "talks with students" that "include[d] religious expression, including prayer," and to avoid "suggest[ing], encourag[ing] (or discourag[ing]), or supervis[ing]" any prayers of students, which students remained free to "engage in." The District also explained that any religious activity on Kennedy's part must be "nondemonstrative (*i.e.*, not outwardly discernible as religious activity)" if "students are also engaged in religious conduct" in order to "avoid the perception of endorsement." In offering these directives, the District appealed to what it called a "direct tension between" the "Establishment Clause" and "a school employee's [right to] free[ly] exercise" his religion. To resolve that "tension," the District explained, an employee's free exercise rights "must yield so far as necessary to avoid school endorsement of religious activities."

After receiving the District's September 17 letter, Mr. Kennedy ended the tradition [of] offering locker-room prayers. He also ended his practice of incorporating religious references or prayer into his postgame motivational talks to his team. [Kennedy] further felt pressured to abandon his practice of saying his own quiet, on-field postgame prayer. Driving home after a game, however, he felt upset that he had "broken [his] commitment to God" by not offering his own prayer, so he turned his car around and returned to the field. By that point, everyone had left the stadium, and he walked to the 50-yard line and knelt to say a brief prayer of thanks.

On October 14, through counsel, Kennedy sent a letter to school officials informing them that, because of his "sincerely-held religious beliefs," he felt "compelled" to offer a "post-game personal prayer" of thanks at midfield. He asked the District to allow him to continue that "private religious expression" alone. Consistent with the District's policy, Kennedy explained that he "neither requests, encourages, nor discourages students from participating in" these prayers. Kennedy emphasized that he sought only the opportunity to "wai[t] until the game is over and the players have left the field and then wal[k] to mid-field to say a short, private, personal prayer." He "told everybody" that it would be acceptable to him to pray "when the kids went away from [him]." He later clarified that this meant he was even willing to say his "prayer while the players were walking to the locker room" or "bus," and then catch up with his team. However, Kennedy objected to the logical implication of the District's September 17 letter, which he understood as banning him "from bowing his head" in the vicinity of students, and as requiring him to "flee the scene if students voluntarily [came] to the same area" where he was praying. After all, District policy prohibited him from "discourag[ing]" independent student decisions to pray.

On October 16, shortly before the game that day, the District responded with another letter. The District acknowledged that Kennedy "ha[d] complied" with the "directives" in its September 17 letter. Yet instead of accommodating his request to offer a brief prayer on the field while students were busy with other activities—whether heading to the locker room, boarding the bus, or perhaps singing the school fight song— the District issued an ultimatum. It forbade Kennedy from engaging in "any overt actions" that could "appea[r] to a reasonable observer to endorse . . . prayer . . . while he is on duty as a District-paid coach." . . .

B

After receiving this letter, Kennedy offered a brief prayer following the October 16 game. When he bowed his head at midfield after the game, "most [Bremerton] players were . . . engaged in the traditional singing of the school fight song to the audience." Though Kennedy was alone when he began to pray, players from the other team and members of the community joined him before he finished his prayer. . . .

On October 23, shortly before that evening's game, the District wrote Mr. Kennedy again. It expressed "appreciation" for his "efforts to comply" with the District's directives, including avoiding "on-the-job prayer with players in the . . . football program, both in the locker room prior to games as well as on the field immediately following games." The letter also admitted that, during Mr. Kennedy's recent October 16 postgame prayer, his students were otherwise engaged and not praying with him, and that his prayer was "fleeting." Still, the District explained that a "reasonable observer" could think government endorsement of religion had occurred when a "District employee, on the field only by virtue of his employment with the District, still on duty" engaged in "overtly religious conduct." The District thus made clear that the only option it would offer Kennedy was to allow him to pray after a game in a "private location" behind closed doors and "not observable to students or the public."

After the October 23 game ended, Mr. Kennedy knelt at the 50-yard line, where "no one joined him," and bowed his head for a "brief, quiet prayer." [A]fter the final relevant football game on October 26, Mr. Kennedy again knelt alone to offer a brief prayer as the players engaged in postgame traditions. While he was praying, other adults gathered around him on the field. Later, Mr. Kennedy rejoined his players for a postgame talk, after they had finished singing the school fight song.

C

Shortly after the October 26 game, the District placed Mr. Kennedy on paid administrative leave and prohibited him from "participat[ing], in any capacity, in . . . football program activities." In a letter explaining the reasons for this disciplinary action, the superintendent criticized Kennedy for engaging in "public and demonstrative religious conduct while still on duty as an assistant coach" by offering a prayer following the games on October 16, 23, and 26. The letter did not allege that Kennedy performed these prayers with students, and it acknowledged that his prayers took place while students were engaged in unrelated postgame activities. Additionally, the letter faulted Kennedy for not being willing to pray behind closed doors.

In an October 28 Q&A document provided to the public, the District admitted that it possessed "no evidence that students have been directly coerced to pray with Kennedy." The Q&A also acknowledged that Mr. Kennedy "ha[d] complied" with the District's instruction to refrain from his "prior practices of leading players in a pre-game prayer in the locker room or leading players in a post-game prayer immediately following games." . . .

While Mr. Kennedy received "uniformly positive evaluations" every other year of his coaching career, after the 2015 season ended in November, the District gave him a poor performance evaluation. The evaluation advised against rehiring Kennedy on the grounds that he " 'failed to follow district policy' " regarding religious expression and " 'failed to supervise student-athletes after games.' " Mr. Kennedy did not return for the next season.

II

A

After these events, Kennedy sued in federal court, alleging that the District's actions violated the First Amendment's Free Speech and Free Exercise Clauses. He also moved for a preliminary injunction requiring the District to reinstate him. The District Court denied that motion, concluding that a "reasonable observer . . . would have seen him as . . . leading an orchestrated session of faith." Indeed, if the District had not suspended him, the court agreed, it might have violated the Constitution's Establishment Clause. On appeal, the Ninth Circuit affirmed [on two separate occasions]. [We] granted certiorari.

III

Now [Kennedy] renews his argument that the District's conduct violated the Free Exercise and Free Speech Clauses of the First Amendment. These Clauses work in tandem. Where the Free Exercise Clause protects religious exercises, whether communicative or not, the Free Speech Clause provides overlapping protection for expressive religious activities. That the First Amendment doubly protects religious speech is no accident. It is a natural outgrowth of the framers' distrust of government attempts to regulate religion and suppress dissent. . . .

A

The Free Exercise Clause [protects] not only the right to harbor religious beliefs inwardly and secretly. It does perhaps its most important work by protecting the ability of those who hold religious beliefs of all kinds to live out their faiths in daily life through "the performance of (or abstention from) physical acts."

Under this Court's precedents, a plaintiff may carry the burden of proving a free exercise violation in various ways, including by showing that a government entity has burdened his sincere religious practice pursuant to a policy that is not "neutral" or "generally applicable." Should a plaintiff make a showing like that, this Court will find a First Amendment violation unless the government can satisfy "strict scrutiny" by demonstrating its course was justified by a compelling state interest and was narrowly tailored in pursuit of that interest.

That Mr. Kennedy has discharged his burdens is effectively undisputed. No one questions that he seeks to engage in a sincerely motivated religious exercise. The exercise in question involves, as Kennedy has put it, giving "thanks through prayer" briefly and by himself "on the playing field" at the conclusion of each game he coaches. Kennedy has indicated repeatedly that he is willing to "wai[t] until the game is over and the players have left the field" to "wal[k] to mid-field to say [his] short, private, personal prayer." The contested exercise before us does not involve leading prayers with the team or before any other captive audience. [At] the District's request, Kennedy voluntarily discontinued the school tradition of locker-room prayers and his postgame religious talks to students. The District disciplined him *only* for his decision to persist in praying quietly without his players after three games in October 2015.

Nor does anyone question that, in forbidding Kennedy's brief prayer, the District failed to act pursuant to a neutral and generally applicable rule. [The] District's challenged policies were neither neutral nor generally applicable. By its own admission, the District sought to restrict Kennedy's actions at least in part because of their religious character. [Prohibiting] a religious practice was thus the District's unquestioned "object." . . .

The District's challenged policies also fail the general applicability test. The District's performance evaluation after the 2015 football season advised against rehiring Mr. Kennedy on the ground that he "failed to supervise student-athletes after games." But, in fact, this was a bespoke requirement specifically addressed to Mr. Kennedy's religious exercise. The District permitted other members of the coaching staff to forgo supervising students briefly after the game to do things like visit with friends or take personal phone calls. Thus, any sort of postgame supervisory requirement was not applied in an evenhanded, across-the-board way. . . .

B

When it comes to Mr. Kennedy's free speech claim, our precedents remind us that the First Amendment's protections extend to "teachers and students," neither of whom "shed their constitutional rights to freedom of speech or expression at the schoolhouse gate." *Tinker* v. *Des Moines Independent Community School District* (1969, Ch. 7, Sec. 7, II, supra). Of course, none of this means the speech rights of public school employees are so boundless that they may deliver any message to anyone anytime they wish. In addition to being private citizens, teachers and coaches are also government employees paid in part to speak on the government's behalf and convey its intended messages.

To account for the complexity associated with the interplay between free speech rights and government employment, this Court's decisions in *Pickering* v. *Board of Ed.* (1968, Ch. 7, Sec. 7 III supra), *Garcetti* v. *Ceballos* (2006, Ch. 7 III supra), and related cases suggest proceeding in two steps. The first step involves a threshold inquiry into the nature of the speech at issue. If a public employee speaks "pursuant to [his or her] official duties," [the] Free Speech Clause generally will not shield the individual from an employer's control and discipline because that kind of speech is—for constitutional purposes at least—the government's own speech.

At the same time and at the other end of the spectrum, when an employee "speaks as a citizen addressing a matter of public concern," [the] First Amendment may be implicated and courts should proceed to a second step. At this second step, our cases suggest that courts should attempt to engage in "a delicate balancing of the competing interests surrounding the speech and its consequences." . . .

Both sides ask us to employ at least certain aspects of this *Pickering-Garcetti* framework to resolve Mr. Kennedy's free speech claim. They share additional common ground too. They agree that Kennedy's speech implicates a matter of public concern. They also appear to accept, at least for argument's sake, that Kennedy's speech does not raise questions of academic freedom that may or may not involve "additional" First Amendment "interests" beyond those captured by this framework. *Garcetti.* At the first step of the *Pickering-Garcetti* inquiry, the parties' disagreement thus turns out to center on one question alone: Did Kennedy offer his prayers in his capacity as a private citizen, or did they amount to government speech attributable to the District?

[It] seems clear to us that Mr. Kennedy has demonstrated that his speech was private speech, not government speech. When Mr. Kennedy uttered the three prayers that resulted in his suspension, he was not engaged in speech "ordinarily within the scope" of his duties as a coach. [The] timing and circumstances of Mr. Kennedy's prayers confirm the point. During the postgame period when these prayers occurred, coaches were free to attend briefly to personal matters—everything from checking sports scores on their phones to greeting friends and family in the stands. We find it unlikely that Mr. Kennedy was fulfilling a responsibility imposed by his employment by praying during a period in which the District has acknowledged that its coaching staff was free to engage in all manner of private speech. . . .

In reaching its contrary conclusion, the Ninth Circuit stressed that, as a coach, Kennedy served as a role model "clothed with the mantle of one who imparts knowledge and wisdom." The court emphasized that Kennedy remained on duty after games. Before us, the District presses the same arguments. And no doubt they have a point. Teachers and coaches often serve as vital role models. But this argument commits the error of positing an "excessively broad job descriptio[n]" by treating everything teachers and coaches say in the workplace as government speech subject to government control. On this understanding, a school could fire a Muslim teacher for wearing a headscarf in the classroom or prohibit a Christian aide from praying quietly over her lunch in the cafeteria. . . .

Of course, acknowledging that Mr. Kennedy's prayers represented his own private speech does not end the matter. So far, we have recognized only that Mr. Kennedy has carried his threshold burden. Under the *Pickering-Garcetti* framework, a second step remains where the government may seek to prove that its interests as employer outweigh even an employee's private speech on a matter of public concern.

IV

A

[The] District argues that its suspension of Mr. Kennedy was essential to avoid a violation of the Establishment Clause. On its account, Mr. Kennedy's prayers might have been protected by the Free Exercise and Free Speech Clauses. But his rights were in "direct tension" with the competing demands of the Establishment Clause. [But] how could that be? It is true that this Court and others often refer to the "Establishment Clause," the "Free Exercise Clause," and the "Free Speech Clause" as separate units. But the three Clauses appear in the same sentence of the same Amendment [A] natural reading of that sentence would seem to suggest the Clauses have "complementary" purposes, not warring ones where one Clause is always sure to prevail over the others.

The District arrived at a different understanding this way. It began with the premise that the Establishment Clause is offended whenever a "reasonable observer" could conclude that the government has "endorse[d]" religion. The District then took the view that a "reasonable observer" could think it "endorsed Kennedy's religious activity by not stopping the practice." On the District's account, it did not matter whether the Free Exercise Clause protected Mr. Kennedy's prayer. It did not matter if his expression was private speech protected by the Free Speech Clause. It did not matter that the District never actually endorsed Mr. Kennedy's prayer, no one complained that it had, and a strong public reaction only followed after the District sought to ban Mr. Kennedy's prayer. Because a reasonable observer could (mistakenly) infer that by allowing the prayer the District endorsed Mr. Kennedy's message, the District felt it had to act, even if that meant suppressing otherwise protected First Amendment activities.

[To] defend its approach, the District relied on *Lemon v. Kurtzman* (1971, Sec. 1 II supra) and its progeny. In upholding the District's actions, the Ninth Circuit followed the same course. And, to be sure, in *Lemon* this Court attempted a "grand unified theory" for assessing Establishment Clause claims. That approach called for an examination of a law's purposes, effects, and potential for entanglement with religion. In time, the approach also came to involve estimations about whether a "reasonable observer" would consider the government's challenged action an "endorsement" of religion.

What the District and the Ninth Circuit overlooked, however, is that the "shortcomings" associated with this "ambitiou[s]," abstract, and ahistorical approach to the Establishment Clause became so "apparent" that this Court long ago abandoned *Lemon* and its endorsement test offshoot. *American Legion* (2019, Supp. to p. 1270 supra). [In] place of *Lemon* and the endorsement test, this Court has instructed that the Establishment Clause must be interpreted by " 'reference to historical practices and understandings.' " *Greece v. Galloway* (2014, sec. 1, IV supra). [An] analysis focused on original meaning and history, this Court has stressed, has long represented the rule rather than some " 'exception' " within the "Court's Establishment Clause jurisprudence." . . .

B

Perhaps sensing that the primary theory it pursued below rests on a mistaken understanding of the Establishment Clause, the District offers a backup argument in this Court. It still contends that its Establishment Clause concerns trump Mr. Kennedy's free exercise and free speech rights. But the District now [says] it was justified in suppressing Mr. Kennedy's religious activity because otherwise it would have been guilty of coercing students to pray. [As] it turns out, however, there is a pretty obvious reason why the Ninth Circuit did not adopt this theory in proceedings below: The evidence cannot sustain it. To be sure, this Court has long held that government may not, consistent with a historically sensitive understanding of the Establishment Clause, "make a religious observance compulsory." *Zorach* v. *Clauson*. [But Kennedy's] private religious exercise did not come close to [impermissible] government coercion. [The] only prayer Kennedy sought to continue was the kind he had "started out doing" at the beginning of his tenure—the prayer he gave alone. He made clear that he could pray "while the kids were doing the fight song" and "take a knee by [him]self and give thanks and continue on." Mr. Kennedy even considered it "acceptable" to say his "prayer while the players were walking to the locker room" or "bus," and then catch up with his team. In short, Kennedy did not seek to direct any prayers to students or require anyone else to participate. . . .

The District responds that, as a coach, Kennedy "wielded enormous authority and influence over the students," and students might have felt compelled to pray alongside him. To support this argument, the District submits that, after Mr. Kennedy's suspension, a few parents told District employees that their sons had "participated in the team prayers only because they did not wish to separate themselves from the team."

This reply fails too. Not only does the District rely on hearsay to advance it. For all we can tell, the concerns the District says it heard from parents were occasioned by the locker-room prayers that predated Kennedy's tenure or his postgame religious talks, all of which he discontinued at the District's request. There is no indication in the record that anyone expressed any coercion concerns to the District about the quiet, postgame prayers that Mr. Kennedy asked to continue and that led to his suspension. Nor is there any record evidence that students felt pressured to participate in these prayers. To the contrary, and as we have seen, not a single Bremerton student joined Mr. Kennedy's quiet prayers following the three October 2015 games for which he was disciplined. On October 16, those students who joined Mr. Kennedy were " 'from the opposing team,' " and thus could not have "reasonably fear[ed]" that he would decrease their "playing time" or destroy their "opportunities" if they did not "participate," As for the other two relevant games, "no one joined" Mr. Kennedy on October 23. And only a few members of the public participated on October 26.

The absence of evidence of coercion in this record leaves the District to its final redoubt. Here, the District suggests that *any* visible religious conduct by a teacher or coach should be deemed [impermissibly] coercive. In essence, the District asks us to adopt the view that the only acceptable government role models for students are those who eschew any visible religious expression. [The] District's suggestion [is] not only that it *may* prohibit teachers from engaging in any demonstrative religious activity, but that it *must* do so in order to conform to the Constitution.

Such a rule would be a sure sign that our Establishment Clause jurisprudence had gone off the rails. In the name of protecting religious liberty, the District would have us suppress it. Rather than respect the First Amendment's double protection for religious expression, it would have us prefer secular activity. Not only could schools fire teachers for praying quietly over their lunch, for wearing a yarmulke to school, or for offering a midday prayer during a break before practice. Under the District's rule, a school would be *required* to do so. It is a rule that would defy this Court's traditional understanding that permitting private speech is not the same thing as coercing others to participate in it. It is a rule, too, that would undermine a long constitutional tradition under which learning how to tolerate diverse expressive activities has always been "part of learning how to live in a pluralistic society." *Lee.* We are aware of no historically sound understanding of the Establishment Clause that begins to "mak[e] it necessary for government to be hostile to religion" in this way.

[Meanwhile,] this case looks very different from those in which this Court has found prayer involving public school students to be problematically coercive. In *Lee*, this Court held that school officials violated the Establishment Clause by "including [a] clerical membe[r]" who publicly recited prayers "as part of [an] official school graduation ceremony" because the school had "in every practical sense compelled attendance and participation in" a "religious exercise." In *Santa Fe Independent School Dist.* v. *Doe* (2000, Sec. 1, IV, supra), the Court held that a school district violated the Establishment Clause by broadcasting a prayer "over the public address system" before each football game. The Court observed that, while students generally were not required to attend games, attendance *was* required for "cheerleaders, members of the band, and, of course, the team members themselves." None of that is true here. The prayers for which Mr. Kennedy was disciplined were not publicly broadcast or recited to a captive audience. Students were not required or expected to participate. And, in fact, none of Mr. Kennedy's students did participate in any of the three October 2015 prayers that resulted in Mr. Kennedy's discipline.

V

Respect for religious expressions is indispensable to life in a free and diverse Republic—whether those expressions take place in a sanctuary or on a field, and whether they manifest through the spoken word or a bowed head. Here, a government entity sought to punish an individual for engaging in a brief, quiet, personal religious observance doubly protected by the Free Exercise and Free Speech Clauses of the First Amendment.

And the only meaningful justification the government offered for its reprisal rested on a mistaken view that it had a duty to ferret out and suppress religious observances even as it allows comparable secular speech. The Constitution neither mandates nor tolerates that kind of discrimination.

[Reversed].

JUSTICE THOMAS, concurring.

I join the Court's opinion because it correctly holds that Bremerton School District violated Joseph Kennedy's First Amendment rights. I write separately to emphasize that the Court's opinion does not resolve two issues related to Kennedy's free-exercise claim.

First, the Court refrains from deciding whether or how public employees' rights under the Free Exercise Clause may or may not be different from those enjoyed by the general public. In "striking the appropriate balance" between public employees' constitutional rights and "the realities of the employment context," we have often "consider[ed] whether the asserted employee right implicates the basic concerns of the relevant constitutional provision, or whether the claimed right can more readily give way to the requirements of the government as employer." *Engquist* v. *Oregon Dept. of Agriculture*, 553 U.S. 591 (2008). In the free-speech context, for example, that inquiry has prompted us to distinguish between different kinds of speech; we have held that "the First Amendment protects public employee speech only when it falls within the core of First Amendment protection—speech on matters of public concern." It remains an open question, however, if a similar analysis can or should apply to free-exercise claims in light of the "history" and "tradition" of the Free Exercise Clause.

Second, the Court also does not decide what burden a government employer must shoulder to justify restricting an employee's religious expression because the District had no constitutional basis for reprimanding Kennedy under any possibly applicable standard of scrutiny. While we have many public-employee precedents addressing how the interest-balancing test set out in *Pickering* applies under the Free Speech Clause, the Court has never before applied *Pickering* balancing to a claim brought under the Free Exercise Clause. A government employer's burden therefore might differ depending on which First Amendment guarantee a public employee invokes.

JUSTICE ALITO, concurring.

The expression at issue in this case is unlike that in any of our prior cases involving the free-speech rights of public employees. Petitioner's expression occurred while at work but during a time when a brief lull in his duties apparently gave him a few free moments to engage in private activities. When he engaged in this expression, he acted in a purely private capacity. The Court does not decide what standard applies to such expression under the Free Speech Clause but holds only that retaliation for this expression cannot be justified based on any of the standards discussed. On that understanding, I join the opinion in full.

JUSTICE SOTOMAYOR, with whom JUSTICE BREYER and JUSTICE KAGAN join, dissenting.

This case is about whether a public school must permit a school official to kneel, bow his head, and say a prayer at the center of a school event. The Constitution does not authorize, let alone require, public schools to embrace this conduct. Since *Engel* v. *Vitale* (1962), this Court consistently has recognized that school officials leading prayer is constitutionally impermissible. . . .

The Court now charts a different path, yet again paying almost exclusive attention to the Free Exercise Clause's protection for individual religious exercise while giving short shrift to the Establishment Clause's prohibition on state establishment of religion. To the degree the Court portrays petitioner Joseph Kennedy's prayers as private and quiet, it misconstrues the facts. The record reveals that Kennedy had a longstanding practice of conducting demonstrative prayers on the 50-yard line of the football field. Kennedy consistently invited others to join his prayers and for years led student athletes in prayer at the same time and location. The Court ignores this history. . . .

Today's decision goes beyond merely misreading the record. The Court overrules *Lemon* and calls into question decades of subsequent precedents that it deems "offshoot[s]" of that decision. In the process, the Court rejects longstanding concerns surrounding government endorsement of religion and replaces the standard for reviewing such questions with a new "history and tradition" test. In addition, while the Court reaffirms that the Establishment Clause prohibits the government from coercing participation in religious exercise, it applies a nearly toothless version of the coercion analysis, failing to acknowledge the unique pressures faced by students when participating in school-sponsored activities. [I] respectfully dissent.

[II.A.]

The Court has been particularly vigilant in monitoring compliance with the Establishment Clause in elementary and secondary schools. The reasons motivating this vigilance inhere in the nature of schools themselves and the young people they serve. Two are relevant here.

First, government neutrality toward religion is particularly important in the public school context given the role public schools play in our society. [Accordingly,] the Establishment Clause "proscribes public schools from 'conveying or attempting to convey a message that religion or a particular religious belief is favored or preferred' " or otherwise endorsing religious beliefs.

Second, schools face a higher risk of unconstitutionally "coerc[ing] . . . support or participat[ion] in religion or its exercise" than other government entities. The State "exerts great authority and coercive power" in schools as a general matter "through mandatory attendance requirements." Moreover, the State exercises that great authority over children, who are uniquely susceptible to "subtle coercive pressure." . . .

Given the twin Establishment Clause concerns of endorsement and coercion, it is unsurprising that the Court has consistently held integrating prayer into public school activities to be unconstitutional, including when student participation is not a formal requirement or prayer is silent. . . .

B

Under [our] precedents, the Establishment Clause violation at hand is clear. [Kennedy] was on the job as a school official "on government property" when he incorporated a public, demonstrative prayer into "government-sponsored school-related events" as a regularly scheduled feature of those events. *Santa Fe.*

Kennedy's tradition of a 50-yard line prayer thus strikes at the heart of the Establishment Clause's concerns about endorsement. [Kennedy] spoke from the playing field, which was accessible only to students and school employees, not to the general public. Although the football game itself had ended, [Kennedy] himself acknowledged that his responsibilities continued until the players went home. Kennedy's postgame responsibilities were what placed Kennedy on the 50-yard line in the first place; that was, after all, where he met the opposing team to shake hands after the game. Permitting a school coach to lead students and others he invited onto the field in prayer at a predictable time after each game could only be viewed as a postgame tradition occurring "with the approval of the school administration."

Kennedy's prayer practice also implicated the coercion concerns at the center of this Court's Establishment Clause jurisprudence. This Court has previously recognized a heightened potential for coercion where school officials are involved, as their "effort[s] to monitor prayer will be perceived by the students as inducing a participation they might otherwise reject." *Lee.* The reasons for fearing this pressure are self-evident. This Court has recognized that students face immense social pressure. Students look up to their teachers and coaches as role models and seek their approval. Students also depend on this approval for tangible benefits. Players recognize that gaining the coach's approval may pay dividends small and large, from extra playing time to a stronger letter of recommendation to additional support in college athletic recruiting. In addition to these pressures to please their coaches, this Court has recognized that players face "immense social pressure" from their peers in the "extracurricular event that is American high school football." *Santa Fe.*

The record before the Court bears this out. The District Court found [that] some students reported joining Kennedy's prayer because they felt social pressure to follow their coach and teammates. Kennedy told the District that he began his prayers alone and that players followed each other over time until a majority of the team joined him, an evolution showing coercive pressure at work.

Kennedy does not defend his longstanding practice of leading the team in prayer out loud on the field as they kneeled around him. Instead, he responds, and the Court accepts, that his highly visible and demonstrative prayer at the last three games before his suspension did not violate the Establishment Clause because these prayers were quiet and thus private. This Court's precedents, however, do not permit isolating government actions from their context in determining whether they violate the Establishment Clause. [Like] the policy change in *Santa Fe,* Kennedy's "changed" prayers at these last three games were a clear continuation of a "long-established tradition of sanctioning" school official involvement in student prayers. . . .

[III.A.]

This case involves three Clauses of the First Amendment. As a threshold matter, the Court today proceeds from two mistaken understandings of the way the protections these Clauses embody interact.

First, the Court describes the Free Exercise and Free Speech Clauses as "work[ing] in tandem" to "provid[e] overlapping protection for expressive religious activities," leaving religious speech "doubly protect[ed]." This narrative noticeably (and improperly) sets the Establishment Clause to the side. The Court is correct that certain expressive religious activities may fall within the ambit of both the Free Speech Clause and the Free Exercise Clause, but "the First Amendment protects speech and religion by quite different mechanisms." *Lee.* The First Amendment protects speech "by ensuring its full expression even when the government participates." Its "method for protecting freedom of worship and freedom of conscience in religious matters is quite the reverse," however, based on the understanding that "the government is not a prime participant" in "religious debate or expression," whereas government is the "object of some of our most important speech." Thus, [the] First Amendment's protections for religion diverge from those for speech because of the Establishment Clause, which provides a "specific prohibition on forms of state intervention in religious affairs with no precise counterpart in the speech provisions." Therefore, while our Constitution "counsel[s] mutual respect and tolerance," the Constitution's vision of how to achieve this end does in fact involve some "singl[ing] out" of religious speech by the government. This is consistent with "the lesson of history that was and is the inspiration for the Establishment Clause, the lesson that in the hands of government what might begin as a tolerant expression of religious views may end in a policy to indoctrinate and coerce." *Lee.*

Second, the Court contends that the lower courts erred by introducing a false tension between the Free Exercise and Establishment Clauses. The Court, however, has long recognized that these two Clauses, while "express[ing] complementary values," "often exert conflicting pressures." [The] proper response where tension arises between the two Clauses is not to ignore it, which effectively silently elevates one party's right above others. The proper response is to identify the tension and balance the interests based on a careful analysis of "whether [the] particular acts in question are intended to establish or interfere with religious beliefs and practices or have the effect of doing so." . . .

B

For decades, the Court has recognized that, in determining whether a school has violated the Establishment Clause, "one of the relevant questions is whether an objective observer, acquainted with the text, legislative history, and implementation of the [practice], would perceive it as a state endorsement of prayer in public schools." *Santa Fe.* The Court now says for the first time that endorsement simply does not matter, and completely repudiates the test established in *Lemon.* Both of these moves are erroneous and, despite the Court's assurances, novel.

Start with endorsement. The Court reserves particular criticism for the longstanding understanding that government action that appears to endorse religion violates the Establishment Clause, which it describes as an "offshoot" of *Lemon* and paints as a " 'modified heckler's veto, in which . . . religious activity can be proscribed' " based on " ' "perceptions" ' " or " ' "discomfort." ' " This is a strawman. [The] endorsement inquiry considers the perspective not of just any hypothetical or uninformed observer experiencing subjective discomfort, but of " 'the reasonable observer' " who is " 'aware of the history and context of the community and forum in which the religious [speech takes place].' " That is because " 'the endorsement inquiry is not about the perceptions of particular individuals or saving isolated nonadherents from . . . discomfort' " but concern " 'with the political community writ large.' "

Given this concern for the political community, it is unsurprising that the Court has long prioritized endorsement concerns in the context of public education. No subsequent decisions in other contexts, including the cases about monuments and legislative meetings on which the Court relies, have so much as questioned the application of this core Establishment Clause concern in the context of public schools. . . .

Despite all of this authority, the Court claims that it "long ago abandoned" both the "endorsement test" and this Court's decision in *Lemon*. The Court chiefly cites the plurality opinion in *American Legion* v. *American Humanist Assn.* (2019, supra Supp. to P. 1270) to support this contention. That plurality opinion, to be sure, criticized *Lemon's* effort at establishing a "grand unified theory of the Establishment Clause" as poorly suited to the broad "array" of diverse establishment claims. All the Court in *American Legion* ultimately held, however, was that application of the *Lemon* test to "longstanding monuments, symbols, and practices" was ill-advised for reasons specific to those contexts. . . .

The Court now goes much further, overruling *Lemon* entirely and in all contexts. It is wrong to do so. [It] is true "that rigid application of the *Lemon* test does not solve every Establishment Clause problem," but that does not mean that the test has no value. [Neither] the critiques of *Lemon* as setting out a dispositive test for all seasons nor the fact that the Court has not referred to *Lemon* in all situations support this Court's decision to dismiss that precedent entirely, particularly in the school context.

C

Upon overruling one "grand unified theory," the Court introduces another: It holds that courts must interpret whether an Establishment Clause violation has occurred mainly "by 'reference to historical practices and understandings.' " Here again, the Court professes that nothing has changed. In fact, while the Court has long referred to historical practice as one element of the analysis in specific Establishment Clause cases, the Court has never announced this as a general test or exclusive focus.

The Court reserves any meaningful explanation of its history-and-tradition test for another day, content for now to disguise it as established law and move on. It should not escape notice, however, that the effects of the majority's new rule could be profound. The problems with elevating history and tradition over purpose and precedent are well documented. For now, it suffices to say that the Court's history-and-tradition test offers essentially no guidance for school administrators. If even judges and Justices, with full adversarial briefing and argument tailored to precise legal issues, regularly disagree (and err) in their amateur efforts at history, how are school administrators, faculty, and staff supposed to adapt? . . .

D

Finally, the Court acknowledges that the Establishment Clause prohibits the government from coercing people to engage in religio[us] practice, but its analysis of coercion misconstrues both the record and this Court's precedents.

The Court claims that the District "never raised coercion concerns" simply because the District conceded that there was " 'no evidence that students [were] *directly* coerced to pray with Kennedy.'" The Court's suggestion that coercion must be "direc[t]" to be cognizable under the Establishment Clause is contrary to long-established precedent. The Court repeatedly has recognized that indirect coercion may raise serious establishment concerns, and that "there are heightened concerns with protecting freedom of conscience from subtle coercive pressure in the elementary and secondary public schools." *Lee.* [In] addition, despite the direct record evidence that students felt coerced to participate in Kennedy's prayers, the Court nonetheless concludes that coercion was not present in any event because "Kennedy did not seek to direct any prayers to students or require anyone else to participate." But nowhere does the Court engage with the unique coercive power of a coach's actions on his adolescent players.

[Having] disregarded this context, the Court finds Kennedy's three-game practice distinguishable from precedent because the prayers were "quie[t]" and the students were otherwise "occupied." The record contradicts this narrative. Even on the Court's myopic framing of the facts, at two of the three games on which the Court focuses, players witnessed student peers from the other team and other authority figures surrounding Kennedy and joining him in prayer. The coercive pressures inherent in such a situation are obvious. . . .

[The] Free Exercise and Establishment Clause[s] are equally integral in protecting religious freedom in our society. The first serves as "a promise from our government," while the second erects a "backstop that disables our government from breaking it" and "start[ing] us down the path to the past, when [the right to free exercise] was routinely abridged." *Trinity Lutheran* (Sotomayor, J., dissenting).

Today, the Court once again weakens the backstop. It elevates one individual's interest in personal religious exercise, in the exact time and place of that individual's choosing, over society's interest in protecting the separation between church and state, eroding the protections for religious liberty for all. Today's decision is particularly misguided because it elevates the religious rights of a school official, who voluntarily accepted public employment and the limits that public employment entails, over those of his students, who are required to attend school and who this Court has long recognized are particularly vulnerable and deserving of protection. In doing so, the Court sets us further down a perilous path in forcing States to entangle themselves with religion, with all of our rights hanging in the balance. As much as the Court protests otherwise, today's decision is no victory for religious liberty. I respectfully dissent.

IV. OFFICIAL ACKNOWLEDGMENT OF RELIGION

P. 1270, at end of note 1:

AMERICAN LEGION v. AMERICAN HUMANIST ASS'N, 139 S.Ct. 2067 (2019), again addressed the issue of public monuments with religious origins and connotations. At issue was the so-called Peace Cross in Bladensburg, Maryland. The cross was planned in 1918 as a memorial to the forty-nine Prince George's County solders who had been killed during the First World War. Finally constructed in 1925, the cross was a 32-foot tall "plain Latin cross" on a stone pedestal located on a traffic island at one end of one of the major highways connecting Washington, D.C., with Annapolis, Maryland. The cross, located on state-owned land and maintained by a state agency, was challenged as a violation of the Establishment Clause, but the Court, in a complex series of opinions, rejected the challenge, and in the process put the final nail in the coffin of the *Lemon* test.

ALITO, J., in an opinion that was mostly the opinion of the Court, noted that the *Lemon* test was especially unsuitable for "cases . . . that involve the use, for ceremonial, celebratory, or commemorative purposes, of words or symbols with religious associations," and that there should be a "presumption of constitutionality for longstanding monuments, symbols, and practices." More particularly, and as in *Salazar v. Buono*, infra, "[many] years after the fact . . . [there is] no way to be certain about the motivations of the men who were responsible for the creation of the monument." And as in *Van Orden*, *supra*, and *McCreary*, *supra*, "the purposes associated with an established monument, symbol, or practice often multiply." Moreover, "just as the purpose for maintaining a monument, symbol, or practice may evolve," so too may the message it conveys. And as a result, he said, the very act of removal may be understood as "aggressively hostile to removal."

Applying these concerns to the case at hand, Alito documented the way in which crosses in general, and not just this cross, had come to represent memorials to soldiers and to bravery. This was similar, he said, to the names of places, and "few would say that the State of California is attempting to convey a religious message by retaining the names given . . . by [the] original Spanish settlers [to] San Diego, Los Angeles, Santa Barbara, San Jose, San Francisco, etc." "The cross is undoubtedly a Christian symbol, but that fact should not blind us to everything else that the Bladensburg Cross has come to represent. For some, that monument is a symbolic resting place for ancestors who never returned home. For others, it is a place for the community to gather and honor all veterans and their sacrifices for our Nation. For others still, it is a historical landmark. For many of these people, destroying [the] Cross that has stood undisturbed for nearly a century would not be neutral and would not further the ideals of respect and tolerance embodied in the First Amendment. [This] Cross does not offend the Constitution."

BREYER, J., joined by Kagan, J., concurred, observing that different considerations might apply to newer monuments in different contexts.

KAVANAUGH, J., also concurred, explicitly emphasizing the way in which the *Lemon* test could not explain the Court's Establishment Clause jurisprudence for the 48 years since it was decided. But KAGAN, J., also concurring with most of Alito's opinion, remained of the belief that although "the *Lemon* test does not solve every Establishment Clause problem, [its] focus on purposes and effects [remains] crucial in evaluating government action in this sphere." THOMAS, J., concurring in the judgment, and describing the *Lemon* test as "long-discredited," reiterated his longstanding resistance to the incorporation of the Establishment Clause and thus its application to the states. "And even if [the Establishment Clause did apply to the states,] this religious display does not involve the type of actual legal coercion that was a hallmark of historical establishments of religion." GORSUCH, J., in an opinion joined by Thomas, J., concurred only in the judgment, insisting that merely being offended by the memorial's presence—"offended observer standing"—was insufficient to confer standing to sue in the first place, but also describing *Lemon* as a "misadventure." GINSBURG, J., joined by Sotomayor, J., dissented, documenting that most war memorials, including most of the World War I memorials, do not contain crosses or other religious symbols, and arguing that "[j]ust as a Star of David is not suitable to honor Christians who died serving their country, so is a cross not suitable to honor those of other faiths who died defending their nation. [By] maintaining the Peace Cross on a public highway, [Maryland] elevates Christianity over other faiths, and religion over nonreligion. [When] a cross is displayed on public property, the government may be presumed to endorse its religious content."

———

The interplay (and tension) among the Free Speech, Free Exercise, and Establishment Clauses was also at issue in *Shurtleff v. City of Boston* (2022, Supplement to p. 1063 supra), described at length above, unanimously concluding that a program allowing largely unrestricted opportunities to raise the flags of private organizations on the plaza in front of Boston City Hall could not constitutionally exclude religious organizations and their flags. Such exclusion, the Court held, not only was not required by the Establishment Clause, but also was not permitted by the Free Speech and Free Exercise Clauses.

2. THE FREE EXERCISE CLAUSE AND RELATED STATUTORY ISSUES

I. CONFLICT WITH STATE REGULATION

P. 1299, at end of footnote 94, insert the following new paragraphs:

Litigation regarding the contraceptive mandate of the Affordable Care Act has continued, with the issue of religious exemptions to the mandate raising numerous statutory issues. In *Little Sisters of the Poor Saints Peter and Paul Home v. Pennsylvania*, 140 S.Ct. 2367 (2020), a Supreme

Court majority reversed a Third Circuit ruling and upheld the statutory authority of the Departments of Health and Human Services, Labor, and Treasury to create exemptions from the contraceptive mandate for employers with religious or moral objections to the mandate's requirements. Writing for the majority, Thomas, J., noted that no constitutional question had been raised in the litigation, and concluded that the plain language of the Affordable Care Act authorized all three departments to create the religious and moral exemptions. In a concurring opinion, Alito, J., joined by Gorsuch, J., argued that the religious exemption was required by the Religious Freedom Restoration Act, and thus would be necessary even apart from the language of the Affordable Care Act. Kagan, J., joined by Breyer, J., concurred only in the judgment, and emphasized that on remand the exemption would have to be measured against the administrative law requirement of "reasoned decisionmaking," and hinted that the exemption in its existing form might not satisfy this requirement. Ginsburg, J., joined by Sotomayor, J., dissented, arguing that the Women's Health Amendment to the Affordable Care Act required that contraceptive services be made available even in the face of a claimed exemption by employers.

Related issues about religion-based exemptions from laws of general application have also arisen in the context of Covid-era vaccination requirements. New York, for example, requires healthcare workers to be vaccinated against Covid. The relevant regulation provides an exemption for medical reasons, but not for those whose objection to vaccination is based on religious principles. In *Dr. A v. Hochul*, 142 S.Ct. 552 (2021), one physician and one oral surgeon sought an injunction against the application of the vaccination requirement to them, claiming that the currently available vaccines depended on abortion-derived cell lines, and thus that being vaccinated would conflict with their religious objections to abortion. After the Second Circuit, in a consolidated appeal from separate District Court rulings, rejected all of the claims, the claimants sought injunctive relief in the Supreme Court. The Court rejected the application for injunctive relief. Justice Thomas would have granted the injunction. Justice Gorsuch, joined by Justice Alito, also would have granted the injunction, and wrote a lengthy opinion in support of that conclusion. Justice Gorsuch would have granted injunctive relief on any of three grounds. First, he argued that that multiple official statements, especially by New York's governor, displayed a hostility to the religious claims and religion, bringing the issue within the ambit of *Masterpiece Cakeshop*. Second, the granting of some exemptions but not religious ones undercut the regulation's assertions of neutrality and general applicability, as per the decision in *Fulton v. Philadelphia* (this Supplement, addition to p.1307 infra). And, third, even were there no hostility, and even if there were no exemptions under the regulatory scheme, Justice Gorsuch argued that New York had not demonstrated the necessity of denying the claimed exemptions, relying here on the arguments he presented in the similar case arising out of Maine's vaccination requirement for healthcare workers, a case that had produced the same outcome and the same Court alignment as in the New York case. *Does v. Mills*, 142 U.S. 17 (2021),

P. 1305, at end of note 2:

Trinity Lutheran, in being about funding for the resurfacing of a religious school's playground, appeared to involve only state support for the non-religious activities of a religious institution. Whether the decision would also permit funding by a government program of general application for those parts of a religious institution that were more closely related to the institution's religious mission remained an open question. That question became less open, however, after the Court's 2020 decision in ESPINOZA v. MONTANA DEPARTMENT OF REVENUE, 140 S.Ct. 2246 (2020).

At issue in *Espinoza* was a Montana program providing a $150 tax credit to those who made donations to organizations awarding scholarships for private school tuition. Under the Montana program, the tax credit was available without regard to whether the private schools that were supported (by the choice of the scholarship recipients) were religious or secular. Although a program allowing such indirect support for religious schools would not, under existing doctrine, run afoul of the Establishment Clause (*Locke; Trinity*

Lutheran), both the Montana Department of Revenue and then the Montana Supreme Court concluded that the program nevertheless violated the "no aid" provision of the Montana Constitution, a provision prohibiting "direct or indirect" public funding of any school, college, or university "controlled in whole or in part by any church, sect, or denomination." The issue before the Court in *Espinoza* was whether excluding religious schools from benefiting from an indirect funding program of general application, as the Montana Supreme Court concluded that the Montana Constitution required, violated the Free Exercise Clause of the First Amendment.

Writing for a 5–4 majority, ROBERTS, C.J., held that Montana's exclusion of schools operated by religious organizations from an otherwise comprehensive program of support for private schools violated the Free Exercise Clause. Relying heavily on *Trinity Lutheran*, the majority concluded that "disqualifying otherwise eligible recipients from a public benefit 'solely because of their religious character' triggered strict Free Exercise scrutiny, and that Montana had not demonstrated that the exclusion served interests "of the highest order" (*Lukumi*) and was "narrowly tailored in pursuit of those interests."

Unlike *Locke*, which involved support for the training of clergy, there was no indication in *Espinoza* that the indirect funding would necessarily wind up supporting explicitly religious activities. But the Court found such a distinction unavailing, and indeed irrelevant, concluding that strict Free Exercise scrutiny was triggered by discrimination based on the religious *status* of an institution, without regard to whether the supported activities—the *use* of the funds—were or were not religious in character.

THOMAS, J., joined by Gorsuch, J., concurred with the majority opinion, but wrote separately to reiterate his view that the Fourteenth Amendment did not incorporate the Establishment Clause. For Justice Thomas, the Establishment Clause was too-often employed to validate what would otherwise be Free Exercise violations, and "unincorporating" the Establishment Clause would remove a frequent obstacle to full realization of Free Exercise values.

ALITO, J., also issued a concurring opinion, detailing the way in which Montana's "no aid" constitutional provision, like those in thirty-eight other states, was modeled after the ultimately unsuccessful attempts in the "Blaine Amendment" proposal of 1876 to amend the United States Constitution. The Blaine Amendment movement, Justice Alito argued, was based on explicitly anti-Catholic sentiments, sentiments arising out of anti-immigrant feelings that were pervasive at the time. This history, Justice Alito suggested, provided the context in which Montana's actions should be viewed, a context highlighting the anti-religious motivations that should even now inform the understanding of "sectarian" in provisions such as that in the Montana Constitution. And GORSUCH, J.'s separate concurring opinion focused on the status/use distinction, arguing that "[t]he right to *be* religious without the right to *do* religious things would hardly amount to a right at all."

GINSBURG, J., joined by Kagan, J., dissented, emphasizing the fact that the Montana Supreme Court had, because it believed that the scholarship program violated the Montana Constitution's no-aid provision, invalidated the entire program. For Justice Ginsburg, this meant that there was no program in place, thus eliminating any possibility of discrimination between secular and sectarian schools. Under the Montana Supreme Court's ruling, she insisted, no one received anything, and thus there could be no claim that secular institutions were receiving benefits or support that sectarian institutions were not. [In his majority opinion, Chief Justice Roberts addressed this argument, maintaining that the Montana Supreme Court's invalidation of the entire program was based on a misreading of *federal* constitutional law, a misreading that the Supreme Court was empowered to correct.]

BREYER, J., also dissented, joined in part by Kagan, J. He objected to an "overly rigid" application of the combination of the Establishment and Free Exercise Clauses, urging the majority to be faithful to the "play-in-the-joints" idea suggested in *Trinity Lutheran*. Applying this more flexible and context-specific approach, Breyer took issue with the majority's focus on the status of the recipient institutions and argued that what should matter was what the institution would *do* with the support. And he saw the Montana situation as one in which the recipient institutions, as in *Locke*, would be using state support "for the inculcation of religious truths" precisely because "religious schools seek generally to inspire religious faith and values in their students."

SOTOMAYOR, J., dissented as well, agreeing with Justice Ginsburg that, with no program in force, there was no extant discrimination and thus no case to decide. And Justice Sotomayor also reprised her dissent in *Trinity Lutheran*, seeing the Montana Supreme Court's decision as amounting to little more than a refusal by the state to "pay for [a] religious practice," a refusal that did not violate the Free Exercise Clause.

P. 1306, at end of note 4, insert the following as new paragraph:

The scope of the so-called ministerial exemption from much of state and federal employment law was expanded at the end of the 2019 Term in *Our Lady of Guadalupe School v. Morrissey-Berru*, 140 S.Ct. 2049 (2020). Although the teacher in *Hosanna-Tabor* had been formally designated by her religious school employer as a "minister," and although she had received considerable religious training, the Court in *Our Lady of Guadalupe* held that neither of these attributes were necessary for the application of the ministerial exemption. Writing for a 7–2 majority, Alito, J., emphasized that the criteria set forth in *Hosanna-Tabor* were not to be understood as a rigid formula, and that the teachers whose employment was at issue in the two consolidated cases had substantial responsibilities for religious education in their respective religious schools. Even though neither was designated as a minister, even though both had been trained in the liberal arts and not in religion, and even though both were involved in teaching non-religious subjects, their actual job duties included a sufficient amount of religious instruction and inculcation to qualify them for the ministerial exemption. Thomas, J., joined by Gorsuch, J., concurred in the Court's judgment and opinion, but wrote separately to emphasize that the religion clauses did not permit the courts to second-guess the good-faith determination by a religious institution of who did or did not qualify as a minister. Sotomayor, J., joined by Ginsburg, J., dissented, charging the majority with having distorted the facts, with granting undue deference to a religious institution's determination of the nature of the employee's responsibilities, and of being insufficiently attentive to the basic principle of *Employment Division v. Smith, supra*, that "religious entities" must "abide by generally applicable laws," especially laws dealing with discrimination in employment.

P. 1306, add to footnote 99:

Note also *Seattle's Union Gospel Mission v. Woods*, 142 S.Ct. 1994 (2022), in which the Court unanimously denied certiorari, but which produced a lengthy statement from Justice Alito, joined by Justice Thomas, respecting the denial of certiorari. While agreeing with the denial of certiorari given the particular procedural posture of this case, Justice Alito suggested that in some future case he would be receptive to the claim that the so-called ministerial exemption might apply to all or at least a much larger number of a religious organization's employees.

P. 1307, as new note after note 5:

6. ***Smith under attack.*** *Employment Division v. Smith*'s basic principle—that the effect on religious practices of regulatory laws of general application that neither single out religion nor result from religious animus will not produce substantially heightened scrutiny—remains standing but continues to be the subject of frontal challenge. *Lukumi* and *Masterpiece Cakeshop* avoided the challenge by finding evidence of hostility to religion, and the Court once again declined to take on *Smith* directly in FULTON v. CITY OF PHILADELPHIA, 141 S.Ct 1868 (2021). At issue in *Fulton* was an arrangement in which Philadelphia contracted with various non-governmental agencies to manage the placement of children with foster families. One of those agencies was Catholic Social Services (CSS), which refused to certify same-sex couples to be foster parents because of CSS's religious beliefs in opposition to same-sex marriage. The City, after an investigation, informed CSS that it would no longer continue the same arrangement as had existed in the past unless CSS agreed to certify same-sex married couples as foster parents on the same terms as it certified opposite-sex married couples. CSS challenged the city's actions as burdening their religious practices and beliefs and as discriminating against CSS because of its religious beliefs, all in violation of the Free Exercise Clause. And although the Court upheld CSS's challenge, it did so without confronting the basic holding of *Employment Division v. Smith*. Rather, the Court unanimously concluded that the City's selective and discretionary method of choosing agencies with which to contract for foster parent placement removed the City's actions from *Smith*'s category of actions and regulations of general applicability. Because the discretionary aspect of choosing foster placement agencies made *Smith* inapplicable, *Smith*'s minimal scrutiny for burdens on religion incidental to laws of general application was not, the Court held, at issue.

Writing for the Court, ROBERTS, C.J., concluded that excluding CSS from the City's foster placement program, being discretionary and not the byproduct of a law or regulation of general applicability, must be examined and evaluated under a "strict scrutiny" standard of review. "[Because the City's] non-discrimination requirement imposes a burden on CSS's religious exercise and does not qualify as generally applicable," those actions "are subject to 'the most rigorous of scrutiny' *Lukumi*." "Because the City's actions are therefore examined under the strictest scrutiny regardless of *Smith*, we have no occasion to reconsider that decision here."

As in *Masterpiece Cakeshop*, Philadelphia argued that a broad and generally applicable anti-discrimination law—here, the Philadelphia Fair Practices Ordinance—made the situation at issue in *Fulton* comparable to that in *Smith*. But the Fair Practices Ordinance applied only to places of "public accommodation," and the Chief Justice's opinion rejected the view that services provided by CSS counted as a public accommodation for purposes of determining the constitutional question whether this was a law of general application in the relevant sense. As a result, the only relevant legal provision remaining was that section of the "standard foster care contract" that allowed the Commissioner of the Department of Human Services to grant exceptions "in his/her sole discretion" to its requirement that providers not reject prospective foster parents because of their sexual orientation. This power to grant exceptions, the Chief Justice concluded, fell squarely within *Smith's* conclusion that a law was not generally applicable "if it 'invite[s]' the government to consider the particular reasons for a person's conduct by providing 'a mechanism for individualized exceptions' " (*Smith*, quoting the opinion of Burger, C.J., in *Bowen v. Roy*, 476 U.S. 693, 708 (1986). And Chief Justice Roberts went on to observe that *Sherbert v. Verner*, 374 U.S. 398 (1963), relied upon by Philadelphia, had also been decided on the same grounds of lack of general applicability by virtue of the availability of individually-assessed exemptions.

Smith having been deemed inapplicable, the Court had little difficulty in applying strict scrutiny and finding Philadelphia's justifications for excluding CSS unavailing. "[T]he City's asserted interests are insufficient. Maximizing the number of foster families and minimizing liability are important goals, but the City fails to show that granting CSS an exception will put those goals at risk. [That] leaves the interest of the City in the equal treatment of prospective foster parents and foster children. We do not doubt that this interest is a weighty one, for '[o]ur society has come to the recognition that gay persons and gay couples cannot be treated as social outcasts or as inferior in dignity and worth.' *Masterpiece Cakeshop*. On the facts of this case, however, this interest cannot justify denying CSS an exception for its religious exercise. The creation of a system of exceptions under the contract undermines the City's contention that its non-discrimination policies can brook no departures."

Justice Barrett, joined by Justice Kavanaugh, issued a concurring opinion joining the majority opinion "in full." But she observed that she found the arguments against *Smith* "more compelling," seeing no reason to treat the Free

Exercise Clause as "offer[ing] nothing more than protection from discrimination." And although Justice Breyer did not join this part of Justice Barrett's opinion, he did join the remainder of her opinion, in which she expressed uncertainty about what might replace *Smith* and agreed that this was not the case to decide "whether *Smith* should be overruled, much less what should replace it."

Justice Alito, joined by Justices Thomas and Gorsuch, concurred only in the judgment, arguing that that the Court's reasons for refusing to consider directly the status of *Smith* were flimsy, and that, in actual practice, the Philadelphia arrangements were indeed the kind of laws of general application to which *Smith* applied. He then went on to argue directly against *Smith,* insisting that it represented a departure from *Sherbert v. Verner, Wisconsin v. Yoder, Hobbie v. Unemployment Appeals Commission*, among others, and that both the history and the constitutional text demanded that the Free Exercise Clause be interpreted in a "straightforward" manner to prohibit the "forbidding or hindering unrestrained religious practices or worship." This interpretation, Justice Alito argued, makes the Free Exercise Clause more than a mere non-discrimination provision, and he claimed that it is an interpretation of the Free Exercise Clause supported by the historical record, a record that Justice Alito set forth in great depth and detail. He also discussed at length the way other provisions of the Bill of Rights had been interpreted to require more than non-discrimination, including, for example, the Sixth Amendment's guarantee of a right to counsel. Were *Smith* to be overruled, Justice Alito argued, it could be replaced with the standard he believed *Smith* replaced: "A law that imposes a substantial burden on religious exercise can be sustained only if it is narrowly tailored to serve a compelling government interest." And he pointed to both the Religious Freedom Restoration Act (RFRA) and the Religious Land Use and Institutionalized Persons Act (RLUIPA) as demonstrating that his proposed test, one similar to that imposed by these statutes, would be both workable and interpretable.

Justice Gorsuch, although joining Justice Alito's opinion, also filed his own opinion concurring in the judgment, an opinion joined by Justices Thomas and Alito. Justice Gorsuch also objected to the Court's refusal to take on *Smith* directly. "To be sure, any time this Court turns from misguided precedent back toward the Constitution's original public meaning, challenging questions may arise across a large field of cases and controversies. But that's no excuse for refusing to apply the original public meaning in the dispute actually before us. Rather than adhere to *Smith* until we settle on some 'grand unified theory' of the Free Exercise Clause for all future cases until the end of time, the Court should overrule it now, set us back on the correct course, and address each case as it comes."

––––––––

If and when (with when being more likely than if) the Court directly address's *Smith*'s vitality and its underlying question of what counts as a law of general application, two recent per curiam decisions on the application of COVID-19 restrictions to religious gatherings appear to signal both the issues and the Court's possible resolution of them. Both SOUTH BAY PENTECOSTAL CHURCH v. NEWSOM, 2021 WL 2250818 (2021) and TANDON v. NEWSOM, 141 S.Ct. 1294 (2021) were per curiam decisions dealing with California's COVID-19 restrictions on gatherings as those restrictions applied to religious services and other religious gatherings. In *South Bay*, the Court, with a complex series of opinions, enjoined by per curiam order California's prohibition on indoor worship services but refused to enjoin the capacity restriction and the restriction on singing and chanting. Justice Gorsuch, joined by Justices Alito and Thomas, would have enjoined all of the restrictions on Free Exercise grounds, and Justice Kagan, dissenting and joined by Justices Breyer and Sotomayor, would have enjoined none of them, believing that California had presented ample scientific evidence in support of its restrictions.

The larger Free Exercise issues were presented more clearly in *Tandon*, which reversed the Ninth Circuit's refusal to enjoin enforcement of California's restriction on household religious gatherings to three households. Because the same restriction also restricted some but not all non-religious household gatherings in the same way, the question was whether the existence of a restriction imposed on the exercise of religion could be considered neutral if it was also imposed on some similar non-religious activities, or if instead the very fact that some nonreligious activities were not so restricted made the regulation a neutral one. Does the existence of similarly regulated secular activity make a restriction on religious activity neutral and general, as the Ninth Circuit concluded, or does the fact that at least *some* secular activities are treated differently from religious activities suffice to make the restriction non-neutral? In other words, what is the relevant comparison group or activity for determining neutrality and generality?

In *Tandon*'s per curiam opinion, the Court rejected the Ninth Circuit's view, concluding that differential treatment between religious activity and some secular activity made the restriction non-neutral, even when there were some secular activities that were treated the same as the religious activities. And so although the California law imposed its three-household limit on many non-religious gatherings as well as on religious gatherings, the Court concluded that the existence of secular activities—many of them commercial—that were not restricted but otherwise similar to the religious activities was sufficient to defeat the claim of neutrality, meaning that strict scrutiny would be applied to the restriction.

Chief Justice Roberts did not join the Court's ruling, believing that injunctive relief was inappropriate at this stage of the proceedings. And Justice Kagan, dissenting and joined by Justices Breyer and Sotomayor, argued that the Court had ignored the empirical evidence that California had offered, evidence supporting its view that the non-regulated secular activities were less of a risk for COVID-19 transmission than the regulated religious and secular activities. For example, she argued, California had offered evidence to support the view that duration of exposure was a COVID-19 transmission risk factor and that religious gatherings involved lengthier time together than, for example, many commercial gatherings and transactions. And thus although the majority and the dissenters agreed in theory that neutrality could be defeated by treating relevantly similar religious and non-religious activities differently, the question here, and one likely to recur, and especially if *Smith* remains controlling, is what is to count as relevantly similar.

CHAPTER 9

EQUAL PROTECTION

■ ■ ■

2. RACE AND ETHNIC ANCESTRY

IV. DE JURE VS. DE FACTO DISCRIMINATION

P. 1454, after *Abbott v. Perez*:

———

In DEPARTMENT OF HOMELAND SECURITY v. REGENTS OF UNIVERSITY OF CALIFORNIA, 140 S.Ct. 1891 (2020), the Court, per ROBERTS, C.J., held that the Department of Homeland Security violated the Administrative Procedure Act (by failing to provide an adequately reasoned explanation for its decision) when it rescinded an order allowing unauthorized aliens who arrived in the United States as children to apply for temporary suspension of removal. At the same time, the Court held that the challengers had not adequately pleaded a claim that the agency acted for racially discriminatory reasons. The plaintiffs had cited no evidence of discriminatory motive by the immediately responsible officials—the Attorney General and the Acting Secretary of the Department of Homeland Security—and statements by President Trump that allegedly manifest hostility to Latinos were "remote in time and made in unrelated contexts." Sotomayor, J., dissented on the equal protection question: "[T]he impact of the policy decision must be viewed in the context of the President's public statements on and off the campaign trail."

V. AFFIRMATIVE ACTION

B. Employment and Government Contracts

P. 1491, at the end of note 1(a):

In *United States v. Vaello Madero*, 142 S.Ct. 1539 (2022), Thomas, J., who had joined the Court's opinion in *Adarand*, expressed "doubt whether it comports with the original meaning" of the Fifth Amendment, but suggested that the result might properly survive on other grounds: "[T]he historical evidence [offers] substantial support for the proposition that [the] Citizenship Clause [of the Fourteenth Amendment] guarantees citizens equal treatment by the Federal Government with respect to civil rights."

3. DISCRIMINATION BASED ON GENDER

II. DIFFERENCES—REAL AND IMAGINED

P. 1516, following footnote 78:

The Court relied on *Geduldig* in *Dobbs v. Jackson Women's Health Org.*, 142 S.Ct. 2228 (2022), Ch. 6, Sec. 2 supra, to reject an argument that prohibitions against abortion trigger elevated scrutiny because they discriminate on the basis of sex: "The regulation of a medical procedure that only one sex can undergo does not trigger heightened constitutional scrutiny unless the regulation is a 'mere pretex[t] designed to effect an invidious discrimination against members of one sex or the other.' " (quoting *Geduldig*).

4. SPECIAL SCRUTINY FOR OTHER CLASSIFICATIONS: DOCTRINE AND DEBATES

I. SEXUAL ORIENTATION

P. 1545, at the end of note 3:

In *Bostock v. Clayton County*, 140 S.Ct. 1731 (2020), the Court, per Gorsuch, J., held by 6–3 that an employer's firing of an employee "simply for being homosexual or transgender" constitutes forbidden discrimination on the basis of "sex" under Title VII of the 1964 Civil Rights Act: "Consider, for example, an employer with two employees, both of whom are attracted to men. The two individuals are, to the employer's mind, materially identical in all respects, except that one is a man and the other a woman. If the employer fires the male employee for no reason other than the fact he is attracted to men, the employer discriminates against him for traits or actions it tolerates in his female colleague . . . . It doesn't matter if other factors besides the plaintiff's sex contributed to the decision."

Alito, J., joined by Thomas, J., dissented, as did Kavanaugh, J. The dissenting opinions stressed that "sex discrimination" and discrimination based on LGBT status are different concepts that reflect different attitudes and motivations. Alito, J., thought it among *Bostock*'s likely consequences that "despite the important differences between the Fourteenth Amendment and Title VII, the Court's decision may exert a gravitational pull" toward subjecting anti-LGBT discrimination to the same elevated scrutiny as sex discrimination in suits alleging constitutional violations.

5. FUNDAMENTAL RIGHTS

I. VOTING

D. "Dilution" of the Right: Partisan Gerrymanders

P. 1608, after the first full paragraph, substitute the following paragraph for *Davis v. Bandemer*, *Vieth v. Jubelirer*, and the Notes and Questions that follow on pp. 1616–19:

In DAVIS v. BANDEMER, 478 U.S. 109 (1986), the Court divided over the test to apply to identify constitutionally forbidden partisan gerrymanders under the Equal Protection Clause. WHITE, J., joined by Brennan, Marshall, and Blackmun, JJ., would have required proof of "intentional discrimination against an identifiable political group and an actual discriminatory effect on that group." POWELL, J., joined by Stevens, J., would have focused on "whether the boundaries of the voting districts have been distorted deliberately and arbitrarily to achieve illegitimate ends." A dissenting opinion, by O'CONNOR, J., joined by Burger, C.J., and Rehnquist, J., would have held that challenges to partisan gerrymanders pose nonjusticiable political questions because the Equal Protection Clause simply "does not supply judicially manageable standards for resolving" them.

The view that challenges to partisan gerrymanders present political questions, which gained the support of a plurality of the Justices in *Vieth v. Jubelier*, 541 U.S. 267 (2004), prevailed, by a vote of 5 to 4, in *Rucho v. Common Cause*, p. 1 of this Supplement. *Rucho*, which you should re-read at this time, states the governing law on the constitutional permissibility of partisan gerrymanders. As you re-read Roberts, C.J.'s, majority opinion, consider what practical difference there is, if any, between its ruling that challengers to political gerrymanders pose nonjusticiable political questions and an "on the merits" conclusion that partisan gerrymanders do not violate the Equal Protection Clause or any other provision of the Constitution.

II. TRAVEL

P. 1641, at the end of note 3:

4. ***Abortion regulation and the right to travel.*** In *Dobbs v. Jackson Women's Health Org.*, 142 S.Ct. 2228 (2022), Ch. 6, Sec. 2 supra, Kavanaugh, J., concurring, posed and answered a question about the scope of the right to travel: "[M]ay a State bar a resident of that State from traveling to another State to obtain an abortion? In my view, the answer is no based on the constitutional right to interstate travel." On which of the branches of the right to travel that the Court distinguished in *Saenz v. Roe* might that judgment

rest? For a discussion of possible arguments based on the dormant Commerce Clause and a structurally grounded right to interstate travel, but one that stops short of Kavanaugh, J.'s clear conclusion, see Richard H. Fallon, Jr., *If* Roe *Were Overruled: Abortion and the Constitution in a Post-*Roe *World*, 51 St. Louis U. L.J. 611, 636–40 (2007).

CHAPTER 10

THE CONCEPT OF STATE ACTION

■ ■ ■

2. "GOVERNMENT FUNCTION"

III. REFUSALS TO FIND "GOVERNMENTAL FUNCTION"

P. 1674, after *Jackson v. Metropolitan Edison Co.*:

———

MANHATTAN COMMUNITY ACCESS CORP. v. HALLECK, 139 S.Ct. 1921 (2019), held that a private entity administering the public access channels on a New York cable system was not a state actor despite having been designated to perform that function by the City of New York. New York state law "requires cable operators in the State to set aside channels on their cable systems for public access" and further "requires that use of the public access channels be free of charge and first-come, first-served. Under state law, the cable operator operates the public access channels unless the local government in the area chooses to itself operate the channels or designates a private entity to operate the channels." For the Time-Warner cable system in Manhattan, New York City designated a private nonprofit corporation, Manhattan Neighborhood Network (MNN), to operate the legally mandated public access channels. After the respondents produced a film critical of MNN and MNN televised it, MNN suspended the respondents from further access to MNN facilities. Respondents then sued, alleging that the public access channels were a public forum and that MNN's actions violated their First Amendment rights.

Per KAVANAUGH, J., the Court, by 5–4, ordered dismissal on the ground that MNN is not a state actor. Although "a private entity may qualify as a state actor when it exercises 'powers traditionally exclusively reserved to the State,'" *Jackson v. Metropolitan Edison Co.*, the function of operating "public access channels on a cable system [h]as not traditionally and exclusively been performed by government. Since the 1970s, when public access channels became a regular feature on cable systems, a variety of private and public actors have operated public access channels, including: private cable operators; private nonprofit organizations;

151

municipalities; and other public and private community organizations such as churches, schools, and libraries." As the Court ruled in *Hudgens* v. *NLRB*, "a private entity who provides a forum for speech is not transformed by that fact alone into a state actor. [G]rocery stores put up community bulletin boards. Comedy clubs host open mic nights."

Nor did it matter that New York City had "designated MNN to operate the public access channels" or that "New York State heavily regulates MNN with respect to the public access channels. [That] the government licenses, contracts with, or grants a monopoly to a private entity does not convert the private entity into a state actor—unless the private entity is performing a traditional, exclusive public function."

Kavanaugh, J., dismissed an alternative contention that MNN was a state actor because it acted in the stead of New York City, which should be regarded as the owner or lessor of the public access channels under applicable New York law. "It does not matter that a provision in the franchise agreements between the City and Time Warner allowed the City to designate a private entity to operate the public access channels on Time Warner's cable system. [N]othing in the franchise agreements suggests that the City possesses any property interest in Time Warner's cable system, or in the public access channels on that system."

SOTOMAYOR, J., dissented: "New York City secured a property interest in public-access television channels when it granted a cable franchise to a cable company. State regulations require those public-access channels to be made open to the public on terms that render them a public forum. The City contracted out the administration of that forum to a private organization. [By] accepting that agency relationship, MNN stepped into the City's shoes and thus qualifies as a state actor.

"[The majority] is wrong in two ways. First, the majority erroneously decides the property question against the plaintiffs as a matter of law. [S]econd, and more fundamentally, the majority mistakes a case about the government choosing to hand off responsibility to an agent for a case about a private entity that simply enters a marketplace. [The] majority's opinion erroneously fixates on a type of case that is not before us: one [such as *Jackson*] in which a private entity simply enters the marketplace and is then subject to government regulation. [But] MNN is not a private entity that simply ventured into the marketplace. It occupies its role because it was asked to do so by the City, which secured the public-access channels in exchange for giving up public rights of way, opened those channels up (as required by the State) as a public forum, and then deputized MNN to administer them." The Court's reliance on prior public function cases was therefore misguided. "[When] the government hires an agent, [that agent is a state actor, regardless of whether the government] hired the agent to do something that can be done in the private marketplace too."

CHAPTER 12

LIMITATIONS ON JUDICIAL POWER AND REVIEW

■ ■ ■

2. STANDING

I. THE STRUCTURE OF STANDING DOCTRINE

P. 1755, at the end of note 6:

(c) The Court denied standing based on a causation analysis in CALIFORNIA v. TEXAS, 141 S.Ct. 2104 (2021), in which the plaintiffs argued that a change in law since the Court's prior cases involving the Affordable Care Act (ACA) rendered the statute facially invalid and therefore unenforceable. In *National Federation of Independent Business v. Sebelius*, 567 U.S. 519 (2012), Ch. 2, Sections 2 and 3, a divided Court held that Congress had no authority under the Commerce Clause to require individuals to purchase health insurance, but it upheld the individual mandate, which was enforced via a penalty payable to the Internal Revenue Service, as a valid exercise of the taxing power. After Congress subsequently reduced the penalty for non-purchase of insurance to $0, two individuals and a number of states sought invalidation of the entire ACA. According to the plaintiffs, the individual mandate could no longer be characterized as a tax, and all of the ACA's other provisions were so interconnected with the mandate that if the mandate was unconstitutional, the other provisions were not "severable" or separately enforceable.

Per BREYER, J., the Court found, by 7–2, that because none of the plaintiffs had standing to bring the action against the Secretary of Health and Human Services and the other defendant executive officials, it need not determine either the continuing validity of the now-unenforceable individual mandate or the severability of the mandate from the remainder of the ACA. Although the individual plaintiffs had alleged injury in the form of costs for the purchase of health insurance, they failed to satisfy the causation prong of the standing test: "Our cases have consistently spoken of the need to assert an injury that is the result of a statute's actual or threatened enforcement." In the absence of any credible threat that the defendants would enforce the mandate to purchase insurance, any harm that the plaintiffs had suffered when they bought insurance was not "fairly traceable" to the defendants.

Breyer, J., then turned to the claims of the plaintiff states, who had alleged that they suffered financial injuries from provisions of the ACA other than the individual mandate. In concluding that they lacked standing to challenge the mandate's validity, Breyer, J., again relied on causation principles. He dismissed the states' claim that the mandate led state residents to enroll in state-operated insurance programs that cost the states money by emphasizing the benefits that those programs provide. "[N]either logic nor intuition suggests that the presence of the minimal essential coverage requirement would lead an individual to enroll in one of those programs that its absence would lead them to ignore," he wrote, when the programs' benefits afforded another possible motive for their actions.

Breyer, J., acknowledged that provisions of the ACA other than the individual mandate imposed costs on the plaintiff states, including those incurred in providing information to residents and furnishing information to the Internal Revenue Service. But "no one" claimed that those other provisions, which "operate independently of" the individual mandate, violate the Constitution. The states' averments thus failed to establish standing to challenge the mandate, which they had not shown to be causally responsible for costs in complying with other provisions.

ALITO, J., joined by Gorsuch, J., dissented. "[T]he individual plaintiffs' claim to standing raise[d] a novel question," he thought, but it did not need to be addressed, since "the States have standing for reasons that are straightforward and meritorious." Alito, J., began his analysis of the states' standing with the premise that they had suffered financial injuries in complying with provisions of the ACA other than the individual mandate. Building on that premise, he further reasoned that if the states were correct (1) that the individual mandate was constitutionally invalid and (2) that other provisions of the ACA could not be severed from it, then the states' financial injuries were "indeed traceable to the mandate." According to Alito, J., the Court had granted standing to plaintiffs mounting facial challenges to statutes on grounds of statutory nonseverability in a number of prior cases and then treated the question of statutory severability as one to be resolved on the merits. That was the correct approach, he argued.

Breyer, J., did not respond the substance of Alito, J.'s, standing analysis, which he characterized as a "novel theory" that was neither argued by the plaintiffs in the lower courts nor presented in the plaintiffs' cert petitions and that "[w]e accordingly decline to consider." Thomas, J., filed a concurring opinion in which he agreed with and elaborated upon the "waiver" argument that Breyer, J., asserted more cryptically and that Alito, J., disputed.

Waiver arguments aside, Alito, J., appears correct that a number of the Court's prior decisions entertaining facial challenges to federal statutes have implicitly relied on a standing-though-nonseverability analysis under which plaintiffs who were directly harmed by one provision of a statute were permitted to argue for facial invalidation based on an alleged defect in another provision of an allegedly non-severable statute. (A recent example is *Seila Law LLC v. Consumer Financial Protection Bureau (CFPB)*, 140 S.Ct. 2183 (2020), Ch. 3 of this Supplement, in which a law firm that suffered harm pursuant to a statute's enforcement provisions was permitted to challenge another provision involving the appointment and removal of the CFPB's Director. Although the Court ultimately rejected the plaintiff's argument that an invalid limitation on presidential removal was not severable from the rest of the statute, it did so only after recognizing the plaintiff's standing to mount the facial challenge.) As Thomas, J., noted in his concurring opinion, however, "this Court has not addressed standing-through-inseverability in any detail, largely relying on it through implications."

When the Court more straightforwardly considers the soundness of the theory of "standing-through-inseverability," it will need to reckon with complex principles of severability and non-severability law that have often provoked sharp divisions among the Justices. For an introduction to some of the central concepts and their relationship to one another, see Richard H. Fallon, Jr., *Facial Challenges, Saving Constructions, and Statutory Severability*, 99 Tex.L.Rev. 215 (2020).

P. 1756, at the end of note 7:

Although courts will not order injunctive relief to redress "past" injuries that are unlikely to be repeated, UZUEGBUNAM v. PRECZEWSKI, 141 S.Ct. 792 (2021), held, per THOMAS, J., that a claim for nominal damages can suffice to establish standing and thus permit an adjudication of the merits of a plaintiff's constitutional claim. *Uzuegbunam* arose from a complaint that a public college and its officials violated the plaintiff's free speech rights to engage in religious proselytization on the college campus. By the time the case reached the Supreme Court, the college had withdrawn the policies that it enforced against Uzuegbunam, and Uzuegbunam was no longer a student at the college. Nonetheless, the Court held, by 8–1, that the plaintiff had alleged injury in fact, caused by the defendants, and that nominal damages would redress his injury: "By permitting plaintiffs to pursue nominal damages whenever they suffered a personal legal injury, the common law"—which provided relevant backdrop for the Court's interpretation of Article III— "avoided the oddity of privileging small-dollar economic rights over important, but not easily quantifiable, nonpecuniary rights."

ROBERTS, C.J., dissented, arguing that the common law cases clearly established only that plaintiffs could sue for nominal damages as a form of relief against ongoing or threatened future harms and that cases involving purely past injuries were different. He also thought that allowing nominal damages for past injuries conflicted with "modern justiciability principles" that authorize suit only when judicial relief will "compensat[e] the plaintiff for a past loss" or prevent "an ongoing or future harm."

P. 1757, after the second paragraph of note 9:

In *June Medical Services LLC. v. Russo*, 140 S.Ct. 2103 (2020), p. 59, *supra*, a divided Court allowed abortion doctors to assert the rights of their patients in challenging a statute that required any doctor who performs abortions to have admitting privileges at a nearby hospital. Dissenting, Alito, J., joined by Thomas and Gorsuch, JJ., argued that conflict-of-interest principles should bar the doctors' assertion of women's rights to challenge a statute ostensibly enacted to protect women's health.

II. CONGRESSIONAL POWER TO CREATE STANDING

P. 1766, at the end of note 2:

The Court clarified and arguably stiffened the "concrete" injury requirement in TRANSUNION LLC v. RAMIREZ, 141 S.Ct. 2190 (2021), another case under the Fair Credit Reporting Act (FCRA), which "requires consumer reporting agencies to 'follow reasonable procedures to assure maximum possible accuracy' in consumer reports and creates a cause of action for "any consumer" whose rights under the Act are violated. The TransUnion case grew out of a product marketed by a major credit reporting firm to alert its customers when consumers had names matching those on a U.S. government list of terrorists, drug traffickers, and other serious criminals. In determining which individuals to flag as "potential match[es]" with names on the government list, TransUnion initially conducted no investigation beyond a comparison of first and last names. Ramirez, who was misleadingly identified as a "potential match" and was rebuffed in his attempt to purchase a car as a result, sued TransUnion for failure to follow the "reasonable procedures" that FCRA requires. He also sought to certify a class of all 8,185 people to whom TransUnion sent a mailing during the period from January 1, 2011, to July 26, 2011, containing the information that their credit files contained alerts flagging them as possible terrorists or serious criminals. Within that seven-month period, however, TransUnion actually disseminated the potential-terrorist alerts with regard to only 1,853 consumers; although its files included alerts concerning 6,332 others, as well, it had not furnished those alerts to any customers within the seventh-month period subject to the parties' factual stipulations.

The Court, per KAVANAUGH, J., held by 5–4 that only the 1,853 individuals about whom false or misleading information was disseminated to TransUnion's customers suffered the "concrete" injury required for Article III standing. "The mere existence of a misleading alert in a consumer's internal credit file" did not constitute a concrete injury in the absence of publication or an analogue. Nor could standing be predicated on the risk that misleading information in the plaintiffs' credit files would be disseminated in the future. Although a risk of future injury will sometimes ground standing to seek injunctive relief, "in a suit for damages, the mere risk of future harm, standing alone, cannot qualify as a concrete harm—at least unless the exposure to the risk of future harm itself causes a separate concrete harm." The Court rejected the argument that credit reports on many of the 6,332 class members who claimed standing were likely sent to creditors outside of the seven-month period for which the parties had stipulated that only 1,853 of the plaintiffs' reports were actually distributed but within the nearly four-year period during which the plaintiffs claimed that TransUnion had violated their rights under FCRA. According to the Court, speculation about probabilities would not suffice; it was the plaintiffs' "burden to prove at trial that their reports were actually sent."

THOMAS, J., joined BREYER, SOTOMAYOR, and KAGAN, JJ., dissented. According to Thomas, J., Founding-era practice that informed the meaning of Article III drew a distinction between whether a plaintiff sued "based on the violation of a duty owed broadly to the whole community" or "asserts his or her own rights." Where a plaintiff sued to enforce a "public right" or a duty to the public as a whole, such as a general duty to obey or enforce the law, the existence of a justiciable case or controversy required a showing of concrete harm. But where a plaintiff sought to enforce a right or duty that was private or personal to her—such as a right to be free from trespass to her land—the plaintiff "needed only to allege the violation. [Courts] typically did not require any showing of actual damage."

In the case before the Court, each of the plaintiffs had "established a violation of his or her private rights," because all of the FCRA provisions under which they sued created "duties [that] are owed to individuals, not to the community writ large." By extending the demand for concrete harm to cases involving congressionally created private rights, Thomas, J., maintained, the Court had adopted an approach "remarkable in both its novelty and effects. Never before has this Court declared that legal injury is inherently insufficient to support standing."

"Even assuming that this Court should be in the business of second-guessing private rights," Thomas, J., thought that the plaintiffs had all pleaded concrete injuries: "[O]ne need only tap into common sense to know that receiving a letter identifying you as a potential drug trafficker or terrorist is harmful. All the more so when the information comes in the context of a credit report, the entire purpose of which is to demonstrate that a person can be trusted." According to Thomas, J., the errors in TransUnion's files created a real risk of disclosure at some time other than within the seven-month period in which TransUnion had disseminated erroneous credit reports involving roughly 25 percent of the plaintiff class. "Twenty-five percent over just a 7-month period seems, to me, 'a degree of risk sufficient to meet the concreteness requirement.'"

KAGAN, J., also filed a separate dissent, joined by Breyer and Sotomayor, JJ., to explain that she "differ[ed] with Justice Thomas on just one matter. * * * In his view, any 'violation of an individual right' created by Congress gives rise to Article III standing." By contrast, the Court had said in *Spokeo*, and she continued to believe, that "Article III requires a concrete injury even in the context of a statutory violation." Nevertheless, she thought that her view would lead to the same result as Thomas, J.'s "in all but highly unusual cases" due to the deference that the courts owed to Congress in determining "when something causes a harm or risk of harm in the real world."

3. TIMING OF ADJUDICATION

I. MOOTNESS

P. 1780, at the end of note 3:

In *New York State Rifle & Pistol Ass'n, Inc. v. City of New York*, 140 S.Ct. 1525 (2020), the Court ruled that a challenge to a New York City ordinance that barred licensed gun owners from transporting their weapons anywhere besides seven firing ranges within the City became moot after New York adopted an amended ordinance that allowed "direct[ ]" transport to and from other gun ranges and second homes. Dissenting, Alito, J., joined by Thomas and Gorsuch, JJ., maintained that because the amended ordinance continued to burden the petitioners' asserted right of "unrestricted access" to gun ranges, the dispute remained live.

In *Uzuegbunam v. Preczewski*, 141 S.Ct. 792 (2021), which arose from a public college's alleged violation of a student's First Amendment rights, the Court held that a claim for nominal damages of one dollar permitted adjudication on the merits even after the claim for injunctive relief became moot. Roberts, C.J., dissented. In the absence of either actual damages or ongoing harm, he thought that mootness doctrine applied.